THE WORKBOATS OF SMITH ISLAND

The Workboats of SMITH ISLAND

PAULA J. JOHNSON

The Johns Hopkins University Press

Baltimore and London

This book has been brought to publication with the generous assistance of the Chesapeake Bay Maritime Museum.

Frontispiece: Deadrise workboats, skiffs, and a scraping boat in profile across the creek at Ewell, Smith Island, 1992.

The Johns Hopkins University Press
2715 North Charles Street
Baltimore, Maryland 21218-4319
The Johns Hopkins Press, Ltd., London

Library of Congress Cataloging-in-Publication Data
Johnson, Paula J., 1954–
   The workboats of Smith Island / Paula J. Johnson.
      p.   cm.
   Includes bibliographical references and index.
   ISBN 0-8018-5484-9 (hc : alk. paper)
   1. Work boats — Smith Island (Md. and Va.)
  I. Title.
  VM351.J63   1997
  623.8'2026'0975518 — dc20   96-32866

A catalog record for this book is available from the British Library.

PHOTOGRAPHS: pp. ii, 5, 21, 40, 62, 69, 76 — Marion E. Warren; p. 4 — courtesy of Elaine Eff; p. 19 — courtesy of Julia Tyler; pp. 23, 38 — Mrs. Lorenzo Somers (courtesy of Mr. and Mrs. Lorenzo "Rooster" Somers); pp. 20, 24, 34 — courtesy of Mr. and Mrs. Morris Goodman Marsh; p. 22 (*right*) — courtesy of Larry Marsh; p. 22 (*left*) — Starke Jett (courtesy of Reedville Fishermen's Museum); p. 44 — courtesy of George M. Butler; p. 58 — courtesy of Virginia Evans; all other photographs by author, those on pp. 52 and 56 — courtesy of Calvert Marine Museum

MAP: p. 2 — Bette G. Bumgarner

DRAWINGS: p. 16 — courtesy of Smithsonian Institution, National Museum of American History; all other drawings courtesy of Smithsonian Institution, National Museum of American History, Transportation Collections: pp. 28–32, 46–50 — Richard K. Anderson Jr.; pp. 17 and 59 — Howard I. Chapelle; p. 60

INVOICE: p. 42 — courtesy of George M. Butler

In memory of Gerald E. Parsons Jr.
whose eye for traditional boats
and affection for the Chesapeake
continue to inspire

CONTENTS

PREFACE

Smith Island, Maryland, has long held a fascination for outsiders. Travel writers, journalists, filmmakers, photographers, authors, poets, scholars, and tourists have all weathered the voyage to Smith Island for various pursuits, personal and professional. Invariably, they come away aiming to convey in words and pictures the complex place that seems so utterly, completely different from the mainstream society that is, geographically speaking, so close.

The lure of such a place is not difficult to fathom. Romantic notions of island living appeal to outsiders who relish an island's remove from the frantic pace and stress of daily urban life. The quality of light surrounding Smith Island and its marshes can be breathtaking, which surely explains the compulsion photographers feel to capture Smith Island scenes on film. Further, most accounts of Smith Island note the "Elizabethan speech" of its people. Elizabethan or no shall be left to the linguists, but the place *is* full of good talkers, fine humor, as well as accents and turns of phrase that both please and puzzle the ear, seeming to speak of another time. Television newscasters, writers and photographers for *National Geographic*, and many, many others have landed on Smith Island for a few days or weeks and brought back glimpses of a place that seems rugged and raw, yet quite appealing.[1]

I came to Smith Island as yet another outsider, representing the State of Maryland and, later, the Smithsonian Institution. My association with the state began in 1989 as a consultant to the Cultural Conservation Program, an office in the Division of Historical and Cultural Programs of the Maryland Historical Trust. This office had been contacted to assist a group of Smith Islanders, led by Frances Kitching (of cookbook fame), who had approached Governor William Donald Schaefer for help in developing an interpretive center for visitors to the island. A number of islanders had become concerned that day-tripping tourists left with little understanding of, or appreciation for, island culture. The head of Maryland's Cultural Conservation Program, Elaine Eff, organized an interdisciplinary team to work with community members in developing an interpretive plan. Historians of architecture and religion, folklorists, material culture specialists, and nautical archaeologists gathered in April 1990 to assess the island's cultural resources and to meet with community members.

At this first meeting, members of the community identified several topics they felt were essential to any presentation about island life: the role of the church, the seafood business, island speech and storytelling, food traditions, and boats. By virtue of field research and exhibition work I had done in southern Maryland, I became the "boat person" for the Smith Island project.[2] In this role, I would work with island watermen and boatbuilders in collecting and presenting information about the island's fleet to a general audience.

As is often the case when working with a community of experts such as Smith Island watermen, it is hard to know just where to begin collecting, organizing, and translating for a general audience the experts' vast knowledge on a subject like workboats. Because boats are so central and basic to Smith Islanders, researching the subject seemed, at first, like asking someone to explain breathing. But with each visit, I became further convinced that the world of workboats at Smith Island merited documentation beyond the project's original scope.

At roughly the same time, I joined the staff of the Smithsonian Institution's National Museum of American History. My new position, as the maritime history specialist in the Division of Transportation, landed me in the former quarters of Howard I. Chapelle, naval architect and eminent historian of American watercraft, who served as the Curator of Transportation from 1957 to 1971. Chapelle's contri-butions to the study of historic American ships and small craft are unparalleled.[3] During his tenure at the Smithsonian, he enhanced the institution's National Watercraft Collection by adding hundreds of his lines plans documenting an astonishing array of American vessel types.[4] Into this context, then, I arrived with research on working vessels at Smith Island already begun. With support from the Division of Transportation and the National Museum of American History, I was able to expand this research with an eye toward adding new documentary materials to the National Watercraft Collection. One result is this study, concerning a particular and significant workboat fleet that is at once unique and in transition, like the community of Smith Island itself.

ACKNOWLEDGMENTS

This project has benefited mightily from the expertise, enthusiasm, and encouragement of many individuals. First and foremost, I wish to thank all the people of Smith Island who gave generously of their time and knowledge. Over the course of this study, Leon and Larry Marsh answered literally hundreds of questions about Smith Island workboats, always with patience and thoughtfulness. They welcomed me and fellow researchers to their Rhodes Point boatyard, where they allowed us to examine vessels out of the water, observe maintenance and repair techniques, and participate in the boat talk that permeates their world. Getting around Smith Island with cumbersome field gear was a perpetual challenge, and Larry often came to our rescue. Without him and his array of vehicles, we might still be hiking through the marsh, swatting swarms of greenhead flies.

Many other islanders went out of their way to be helpful, and to them I am deeply grateful: Julian "Juke" Bradshaw Sr.; Jesse and Mitzi Brimer; Louise Brimer; Eddie A. Evans; Elmer "Junior" Evans; Pastor Edward Gladden; Daniel and Dorothy Harrison; Mike and Yvonne Harrison; Frances and Ernest Kitching; David Laird; Terry and Donna Jean Laird; Morris, Brenda, and Darlene Marsh; Dwight and Mary Ada Marshall; Haynie Marshall; Tim Marshall; Lorenzo "Rooster" and Eileen Somers; Julia Tyler; Maude Whitelock; the boatyard crew, including Mike Marsh and Bobby Gene Tyler; and members of the Crisfield and Smith Island Cultural Alliance. I owe special thanks to Jennings and Edwina Evans and their son Ben (and pooch Midnight) for evenings spent in conversation in their home, and to everyone at Ruke's Restaurant for preparing and serving one excellent crabcake after another. Last but not least, I am indebted to Janice and Bobby Marshall, of Tylerton, for their generous hospitality and heartfelt good humor.

Initial field research was coordinated by Elaine Eff, director of the Cultural Conservation Program of the Maryland Historical Trust and supported through grants from the trust, the Maryland Humanities Council, and the Maryland State Arts Council. The American Folklife Center at the Library of Congress lent us professional recording equipment. Once the project was underway, the Division of Transportation and the Research Opportunities Fund of the Smithsonian Institu-

xii

tion's National Museum of American History supported fieldwork and documentation. I owe special thanks to Richard K. Anderson Jr., documentation consultant, for his excellent work in the field, taking the lines off two workboats. His resulting drawings of the workboats *Darlene* and *Louise B.*, which help illustrate this study, speak volumes for his craft. I also wish to tip my hat to Marion Warren, who kindly allowed me to use several of his fine photographs, and to Bette Bumgarner, who drew the map of the Smith Island area.

Many friends and colleagues read early drafts of this manuscript and offered excellent suggestions for improvement. Among them are George G. Carey, Melvin A. Conant, Richard J. S. Dodds, Elaine Eff, Paul F. Johnston, Steven Lubar, Orlando Ridout V, and Quentin Snediker. Special thanks are due David A. Taylor, who was always willing to discuss one more idea, one more boat, one more draft. Larry Chowning was helpful at crucial points throughout this study, especially in regard to Virginia-built boats. For insight into such vessels, I am also grateful to George M. Butler, of Reedville, Virginia, as well as to Alicia Rouverol, Starke Jett, and the Reedville Fishermen's Museum. Many thanks are due John Valliant and the Chesapeake Bay Maritime Museum for helping to bring this publication to fruition. And, finally, I owe special thanks to my husband, Carl Fleischhauer, who offered encouragement at every turn and never tired of hearing about the boats and people I encountered at Smith Island. While I intended to heed the sound advice of my readers and consultants, any errors that remain are entirely my own.

THE WORKBOATS OF SMITH ISLAND

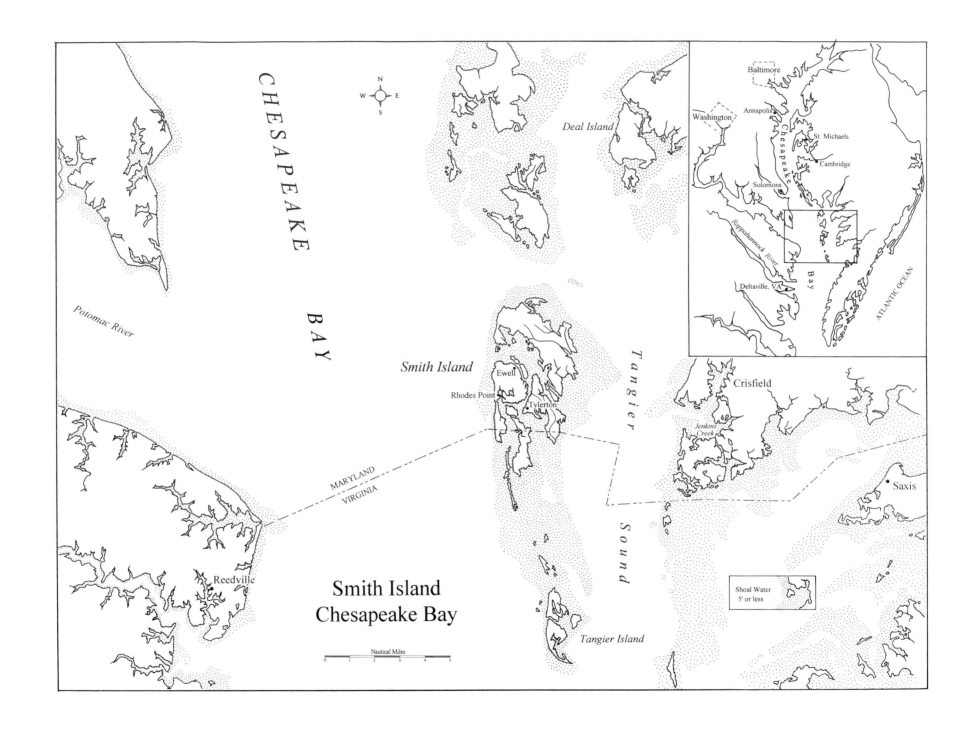

SMITH ISLAND · MARYLAND

Where Everybody Needs a Boat

The Chesapeake Bay and its extensive network of navigable tributaries provided an effective route for transportation, commerce, and communication well into the twentieth century. Among the vessel types built to suit local water conditions and needs—from transport to seafood harvesting—were log canoes, brogans, bugeyes, skipjacks, schooners, and sailing skiffs, to name just a few.[1] With the development of good land transportation systems in this century, the significance of the bay to everyday transport and small-scale commerce has diminished steadily. In turn, the importance and diversity of watercraft in the region has declined as well.

Yet there is one place in Maryland where boats are still of primary importance to every single resident. At Smith Island, boats are still indispensable, varied, and valued. Located twelve miles offshore from Crisfield on the lower Eastern Shore, Smith Island is really a cluster of marshy islands nestled in the Chesapeake, straddling the Maryland-Virginia state line. The only inhabitable part of the marsh lies in Maryland, and Smith Island has the distinction of being that state's only populated offshore island. The 1990 census tallied 453 residents, most of whom are descendants of the Evans, Tyler, Marsh, Bradshaw, and Thomas families, who settled there in the eighteenth century.[2]

Since the early nineteenth century, when the waterborne evangelist Joshua Thomas carried the doctrine of Methodism to people in the remotest villages of the region, Smith Island has been a

4

Rev. Edward Gladden, Eddie A. Evans (*standing*), and Elmer "Tank" Evans traveling by boat to church in Tylerton from Ewell.

stronghold of the Methodist faith.[3] Today the church continues to be a guiding force in all aspects of community life, serving as local government as well as moral anchor. An abiding faith that the Lord will provide undergirds daily life and the island's main occupation, the "water business," or the annual round of harvesting seafood resources from the Chesapeake Bay. Generations of Smith Islanders have depended entirely on the water business for their livelihood, and the community includes some of the bay's most proficient watermen. Retired waterman Jennings Evans described the importance of the seafood business in the most basic of terms: "The bay rules our lives. Everybody's after a crab here. You can have all the education in the world, but if you can't tell a peeler [a molting crab], you ain't nothing here."[4]

Smith Island watermen and their families live in one of three villages—Ewell, Rhodes Point, or Tylerton—built on the highest points of land in the marsh. Ewell and Rhodes Point are linked by two miles of paved road, which snakes through the marsh and offers islanders with auto-

mobiles a small measure of mobility. Tylerton, however, has neither roads for vehicles nor cars, but is laced with lanes for foot traffic, bicycles, and golf carts, the last being the preferred mode of carrying goods home from the pier.

Rhodes Point resident Larry Marsh knows how important boats are to his neighbors. He and his father, Leon, run Smith Island's only boatyard, L. Marsh & Son, in Rhodes Point, where most workboats are brought for repair and seasonal maintenance. Larry Marsh explained:

The people of Smith Island need their boats. They depend on their boats to make their living. They depend on their boats to go back and forth to Crisfield when they need to go, if they don't catch the ferry over. And they use their boats to sport around in on weekends, like on Sundays when they're not using them [for work]. They'll just take baskets and barrels or whatever's in their way out of them, and they use them to sport around in. . . . That's what keeps Smith Island going, these boats these people have around here. It's the only way.

Boats are indeed essential, being virtually the only mode of transportation to and from the mainland for people in all three communities. Every Smith Islander depends on the ferries, the mail boat, or the school boat, which make daily runs between Smith Island and Crisfield.[5] Practically everything has to be imported to the island—groceries, furniture, appliances, and all building materials for homes, outbuildings, and boats. Only local seafood (crabs, oysters, and fish), pomegranates and figs (which grow profusely on the island), and pet cats (who thrive on seafood scraps) do not have to be ferried in from the mainland. These passenger boats and ferries—the islanders' lifelines—are modern fiberglass or steel-hulled power vessels, manufactured by nationally known boatworks and designed to carry people and goods efficiently. They operate on a fixed schedule, which exerts considerable influence over the way Smith Islanders order their daily lives.

As important as the ferries, mail boat, and school boat are to everyone in the community, however, they do not domi-

nate the island's cultural landscape. Rather, the watermen's workboats, which rim the harbors, reveal far more of the island's true character. One is struck by the sheer number of workboats as well as the variety of workboat types in use at Smith Island. This, coupled with the apparent lack of the sort of recreational vessels that populate most Chesapeake

Smith Islanders aboard the *Capt. Jason*, one of the passenger ferries that make daily trips to Crisfield, on the mainland.

ports, makes the fleet unique in Maryland. Every Smith Island waterman has at least one workboat, many have two, and some have three, each for different pursuits. Jesse Brimer Jr., of Ewell, explained, "I have three boats. I have one for crabbing, one for oystering, and one . . . small skiff, just for, you know, fooling around in."

In this respect, there is a remarkable continuity with the Smith Island fleet of a century ago. In 1884, when Henry Hall prepared his *Report on the Ship-Building Industry of the United States*, for the Tenth U.S. Census, he observed:

The islands on the Maryland shore became densely populated early in the history of settlement, especially Smith's, Deal's, and Tangier's islands. From the necessity of their position the people were obliged to have the means of crossing the water, and from the earliest times they bought or made for themselves wooden canoes, each hewn from the trunk of one tree. Almost every family owned one, two, and even three boats, and the men were out in them the greater part of the time, taking the daily meal of fish for the family, traveling to and fro, or sailing off to market somewhere with a canoe loaded down with oysters and fish. A great deal of general trading took place in these boats. The inhabitants of the islands went to church in them on Sundays, and in fact the whole population, white and black, were used to owning and handling canoes, and knew how to make them.[6]

Older Smith Islanders recall when sailing bugeyes, skipjacks, and bateaux populated their harbors, reflecting the vigor of the bay's commercial seafood industries. In fact, the water business *has* kept Smith Islanders and their communities alive for generations. In the last several years, however, working the water has become increasingly difficult. The cadence of the seasonal round—harvesting crabs in summer and oysters in winter—has faltered as the bay's oyster industry has virtually collapsed.[7] Many Smith Islanders admit that crabbing is all that's left; their living is earned from May to October. "Summer is the time when you have to make your money, or you go without, really," declared Jennings Evans. "Islanders have learned to be like squirrels. . . . Any-body that's been in this long enough has to learn how to save their nuts, you know. They gather 'em when the weather's nice and they save a little bit for the winter-time, you know. So the summer is the most important part, really, and if you miss the summer, economically you're out of it."

As the economic realities of the water business bear down on Smith Island, many watermen face an uncertain future. Some young men have settled into mainland jobs, abandoning the occupation for which they prepared all their lives. Older watermen find themselves thinking about how to shave the costs of staying in business, which usually involves getting rid of a vessel or extending the life of an old wooden one by any means available. It rarely means investing in a new boat.

Such downward trends in the water business will surely exact a toll on the number and variety of vessels in the Smith Island fleet. In light of this gloomy prospect, and because Smith Island is the only community in Maryland where everybody truly needs a boat, I began a general "census" of Smith Island watercraft after one of my early visits to the island. The survey was designed to determine basic information about boats in the island's three communities, such as: how many boats of what types were in use; where and when boats had been built; the materials used in construction; the range of purposes to which vessels were put; and commentary by individual owners concerning a vessel's qualities or shortcomings.

The boat census, conducted during several visits between 1991 and 1993, revealed nearly 300 boats at Smith Island, including 146 workboats, 136 skiffs, and 17 specialized vessels such as the ferries, school boat, and pleasure craft (see Appendix A). The majority of boats fell into the three broad categories identified by Jesse Brimer Jr.: crab-scraping boats, larger deadrise workboats (typically used for oystering or crab potting), and skiffs. The wide variety of designs within these general types reflected the use of different construction materials (wood, fiberglass, or a combination thereof) as well as different approaches to boat design by various builders. There was also a considerable range to the age of vessels in the Smith Island fleet, with some nearing their sixtieth year in service and a few approaching their first anniversary. In addition, the fleet reflected individual watermen's ideas about how boats should be named, painted, equipped, and maintained.

Over the course of several visits to the island, I conducted further research to gain a broader understanding of the cultural context of workboats in this island community. This research involved conducting tape-recorded interviews with watermen, photographing boats in and out of the water, and speaking informally with a number of islanders about boats and the water business. Among the topics most vigorously pursued were: how boats are acquired, named, and used; by whom boats are built and repaired; how builders learned their craft and developed their own distinctive models for particular vessel types; the process of building boats; the roles of tradition and innovation in workboat design and construction; how vessels suit the particular work to which they are put; how individual watermen arrange their boats' work spaces to reflect their own working style; terminology pertaining to watercraft and the water business; and the future of the Smith Island workboat fleet.[8]

During one or another of these visits, it became clear that in-depth documentation of representative vessel types was warranted. Because wooden workboats are complex, multifaceted forms, verbal descriptions and photographs simply cannot reveal their true lines or the various details of their construction. Since traditional boatbuilders in the Chesapeake region do not design and build using blueprints or plans, we had to "take the lines" off the vessels ourselves. Under the expert guidance of documentation consultant Richard K. Anderson Jr., two workboats were recorded in detail—*Darlene*, a crab-scraping boat, and *Louise B.*, a round-stern deadrise.[9]

Why, out of the scores of vessels at Smith Island, were these two workboats chosen? Neither is Smith Island's most historically significant boat; that honor would likely go to the venerable *Eleanor White*, built in 1928, and one of the oldest wooden-hulled tankers (known locally as the "gas boat") registered by the U.S.

The crab-scraping boat *Darlene* at Morris Goodman Marsh's crab shanty. The shanty, where
Marsh and his son Allen shed out peelers, is
accessible only by boat.

Coast Guard. Another contender for historical significance is *J. C. Drewer*, built in 1929 and one of the last oyster buy-boats to operate on the bay. But the boats *Darlene* and *Louise B.* are significant in other ways. First, they are excellent examples of two workboat types of critical importance to Smith Islanders and their water business. Second, both vessels are currently in use and well maintained. And third, each displays features of hull construction that are at once typical and distinctive: they are typical of traditional Chesapeake-style boatbuilding, but distinctive in that these construction techniques are rarely practiced in the region anymore. Such construction details in themselves are worthy of documentation.

Equally important, however, is that both boats are associated with exceptional people—builders and owners—who know them inside and out and who were articulate and enthusiastic about sharing that knowledge. The Smith Island project provided an opportunity to collect information about workboats from the very people who could tell us the most about

them. So often such first-hand knowledge of an artifact is just not available; the builders and users are no longer living or have remained anonymous. Such has been the case with many studies of traditional boats, where the chief concern has been technical recording of a vessel's lines, without serious attention to the broader cultural context of which the boat is but a part. By combining technical and ethnographic documentation, greater understanding of and appreciation for the world of workboats at Smith Island is possible.[10]

"A boat that was better than the next boy's" Ask any adult male at Smith Island to describe his boat and he's apt to say, "Which one?" Besides owning multiple vessels, most watermen still recall every boat they have ever owned with such clarity that these boats—some from the distant past—come to life when described by their former owners. For young boys growing up at Smith Island, getting a boat has always been a rite of passage, the means by which they begin acquiring

the skills and competitive edge needed for a life on the water.[11] A boat is the essential tool for entry into the island's premier occupation, the water business. Eddie A. Evans, a waterman in his mid-fifties, recalled his first boat and what it meant to him:

Well, . . . when I was a small kid, I always had a desire to grow up, naturally, like most children do, to be like their father. . . . My father and grandfather was with me like anybody else. . . . They were a role model with me, and what they did enticed me. I never cared to go to school if I could get out and work on the water. I always had a desire, from a very early age, to have my own boat and just be my own boss. Now, at that time you didn't look at it as being your own boss; it was more or less the freedom part of it.

I would say that when I was no more than nine year old, I had my first skiff, which was a big thing for us at that age. It's more or less like a kid today when you get sixteen and you get your first automobile or something. It was really a big deal with us when we got our first skiff. Probably didn't

Bobby Marshall's workboat, *Robin J.*, is prominently featured on the yard sign outside the Marshalls' home in Tylerton. The boat is named for Bobby and Janice Marshall's daughter.

cost over thirty or forty dollars. Didn't have a motor on it. But at that age, we could take that skiff here in the shallows all around the island with a sail on it. We were always rigging sails on it, and it was something that your parents pretty well let you do your own thing. If you wanted to put a funny-looking sail on it, that was fine.

It was your boat. Like I say, they didn't have motors at that time like they do now, and you cut down on the danger at that age quite a bit by not having motors. They just weren't available. So I guess that's the reason that our parents more or less give us the freedom that they did to do what we wanted with these boats. And they're just small boats, . . . 14-, 16-foot, and you could shove 'em just as easy as you wanted with a paddle. And pretty well every kid around here, when they got eight, ten year old, in between there, had a skiff of some type. Now, some was fortunate enough to have new ones, some was lucky enough for to be able to find one that somebody had throwed away and they'd fix it up and whatever. But we were always just messing around with these type of skiffs, rigging 'em like our fathers' boats and what have you, and it was a lot of fun. But it also built the desire into you to be competitive, because you always wanted a boat that was better than the next boy's that was your age, and you were trying to do something different than he was or trying to make it go faster and things of that nature. So that's basically what I remember, as I was growing

Louise Brimer with her namesake, the round-
stern workboat, *Louise B.*, 1993.

WHERE EVERYBODY NEEDS A BOAT

up, of really getting this desire to be a waterman.

Gender roles at Smith Island are well defined according to custom. This important rite of passage—getting one's first boat—applies to island boys. According to the prevailing view, it is the boys who will become watermen, who will need to know about boats and become competent in the ways of the water business. While island women need and depend on boats, they are not socialized into the occupation. They are not encouraged to acquire skills for working on the water, "messing around" in boats, or developing the waterman's competitive spirit. Some women view the water as a barrier to mobility, while a few admit to being anxious about crossing the sound. Still, a number of girls and women, especially those who live in remote Tylerton, have learned to operate skiffs powered by outboard motors.[12]

All islanders—male and female, young and old—understand the crucial role of workboats to the economy and culture of Smith Island. Workboats occupy an important place in the hearts, minds, and identities of their owners. Images of workboats past and present not only decorate Smith Island yards but adorn grave markers of former captains as well. In a sense, the workboats are like members of the community. Writing about his childhood in Crisfield, Glenn Lawson recalled, "Strange, I thought, how I attributed human characteristics to a boat, especially to a big, wooden boat. I supposed I had learned that as a child growing up in a waterman's home. There, the boat was always treated, and even spoken of, like it was another member of the family. A very important member of the family, at that."[13]

Likewise, in speaking about his skipjack, *Ruby G. Ford*, Capt. Edward Harrison pointed out: "Being on a boat all your life, that boat becomes a part of you. Helps raise your family. For her size, she was about as smart a boat as there was on the Bay."[14]

Despite being the domain of men, workboats on Smith Island, as elsewhere in the Chesapeake, are typically named after female family members.[15] There is, however, the occasional *Footloose, Rock-a-Little,* and *Last Call,* usually the vessels of younger watermen. And a few names require interpretation. As I puzzled over the meaning of a boat named *Bartimaeus II,* in the harbor at Ewell, the boat's owner, Jeff Evans, explained that Bartimaeus was a blind man in the Bible whose sight was restored.[16] Evans himself had lost his sight several years earlier after becoming ill. Following an operation, he regained his vision, and he must have felt he was something of a second Bartimaeus. Among some Chesapeake watermen it is considered bad luck to change the name of one's boat.[17] Whether this taboo crossed Evans's mind is not known, but, in a sense, he did not abandon the spirit or intent of the boat's original name. His father had named the boat *Jeff,* in honor of his son; after the death of his father, Jeff Evans simply renamed the boat to reflect his new identity as *Bartimaeus II,* another blind man healed.

The majority of workboats at Smith Island form a roster of female community members past and present. Among the workboat fleet are:

BOAT	OWNER	RELATIONSHIP
Miss Peggy	Darren Evans	mother
Miss Brenda	Allen Marsh	mother
Robin J.	Bobby Marshall	daughter
Miss Maxine	Ed Landon	wife
Miss Norma	Julian "Juke" Bradshaw Sr.	wife
Miss Sherry	Elmer "Junior" Evans	daughter
Ma Dorothy	Daniel Harrison	wife
Miss Charlotte	Ruthman Dize	wife
Maria Rose	Kevin Marshall	sister
Jessica Lynn	Jesse Brimer Jr.	daughter
Darlene	Morris Goodman Marsh	daughter
Louise B.	Jesse Brimer Jr.	mother

As in maritime communities the world over, all boats at Smith Island, even those with names like *Darrell-Dale* (named for two sons) or *Smith Bros.* (named for male siblings), are referred to as "she."[18] This way of speaking can cause some confusion if one does not listen carefully. Telling about how he got his new boat, Jennings Evans explained that his first boat was leaking around the stern so he took her to the marine railway where a similar boat, *Marge*, had just been repaired and was for sale. On the spur of the moment, Evans decided to get rid of the old boat and buy the new one, or, as he put it, "So I went home with *Marge*. She's about the same age as the other one."

Wooden crab-scraping boat built by Michael Harrison Sr. for his son Mike, in Ewell, 1989. The scrapes lean against the awning sticks. Also note the "booby house" forward, which provides partial covering over the deck. Harrison recalled that as a youngster accompanying his father to the scraping grounds, he spent many hours staying dry and sleeping under the booby house.

CRAB-SCRAPING BOATS

Crab-scraping boats, the most distinctive craft at Smith Island, are perfectly suited to local conditions and their specific purpose: harvesting peelers and soft crabs in the shallow waters of Tangier Sound. Their deadrise (V-shaped) hull is sharp forward and nearly flat aft, producing a vessel that draws only about 18 inches of water. Scraping boats range in size from 24 to 30 feet, and are characteristically broad of beam (typically equal to one-third the length) and low of freeboard (approximately 18 inches at the stern). They are undecked and cabinless, although some, especially older models, have a removable "booby house" forward that provides storage for miscellaneous gear, such as oilskins. In the heat of summer many watermen rig an awning over the open work space to protect the crabs and themselves from the relentless summer sun.

Smith Island watermen use scraping boats to harvest blue crabs (*Callinectes sapidus*) in various stages of molting, the process a crab undergoes when shedding its shell to grow. "Peelers" are crabs that are within days or hours of shedding; "busters" are in the process of shedding, or busting out of their shells; and "soft crabs" have just emerged from their old, hard shells. Soft crabs are entirely defenseless and thus are vulnerable to predators of all types, including watermen. The soft crab's new, larger shell remains soft for just a few hours; once it starts to harden, the crab becomes known as a "buckram" and is no longer marketable as a soft crab. Considered a delicacy by people the world over, soft crabs are the most valuable com-

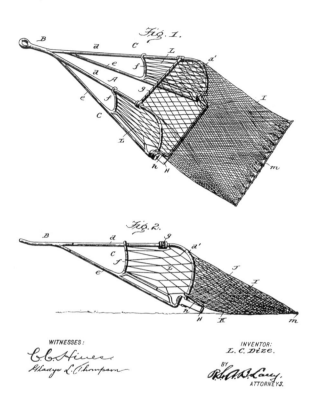

Smith Island native Lewis C. Dize patented this scrape bag design in 1898. His improvements included a spreader frame to keep the mouth of the net open and a stiffening cord to "prevent parting of the strands under strain and undue bulging out of the net at one side of its center" (United States Patent Office, patent no. 614,706).

mercially, or, as waterman Julian "Juke" Bradshaw Sr. remarked, "That soft crab, he's the one you get paid for."

When crabs are preparing to molt around Smith Island they seek cover in the vast beds of eelgrass, which proliferate in Tangier Sound, the portion of the bay lying between the mainland and the islands of Smith, in Maryland, and Tangier, in Virginia. The scraping boat's shallow draft is ideal for gliding through this "good crabbing bottom," pulling the harvesting gear, called (what else?) a scrape. The gear is simple, consisting of a toothless iron dredge and a long mesh bag towed alongside the boat for a few minutes at a time, bringing up wads of eelgrass in which crabs and other creatures are hidden. The boat's low freeboard facilitates lifting and emptying the gear, which is done by hand when two scrapes are towed, port and starboard. (If a winch, or mechanical hauler, is used to lift the gear, only one scrape can be employed, according to current Maryland law.) The vessel's sharp V-bottom forward plus its beamy hull provide a stable working platform, essential for lifting the gear and

emptying it on the vessel's wide washboards. Smith Islanders have equipped their scraping boats with live boxes of various sorts, designed to keep the highly perishable peelers, busters, and soft crabs alive until they are unloaded at the crabber's shedding shanties (in the case of peelers and busters) or packed for market (in the case of soft crabs).

Present-day crab-scraping boats are updated versions of the sail-powered scrapers described by Howard I. Chapelle in his 1943 article, "Chesapeake Bay Crabbing Skiffs." Chapelle deemed sailing crab-scraping boats as "the most popular small work boat from Tilghman's to Tangier," after the log canoe, and noted, "These yacht-like boats were neither true skiffs nor bateaux but combined the features of both. . . . In every respect, they were reduced scale copies of the larger oyster dredging bateaux, or 'Skipjack,' except that the Crabber had no permanent cabin trunk and was usually half-decked. . . . Today, this type is rapidly disappearing and the remnants of a once numerous fleet are wearing out at Deal's Island or nearby crabbing centers."[1]

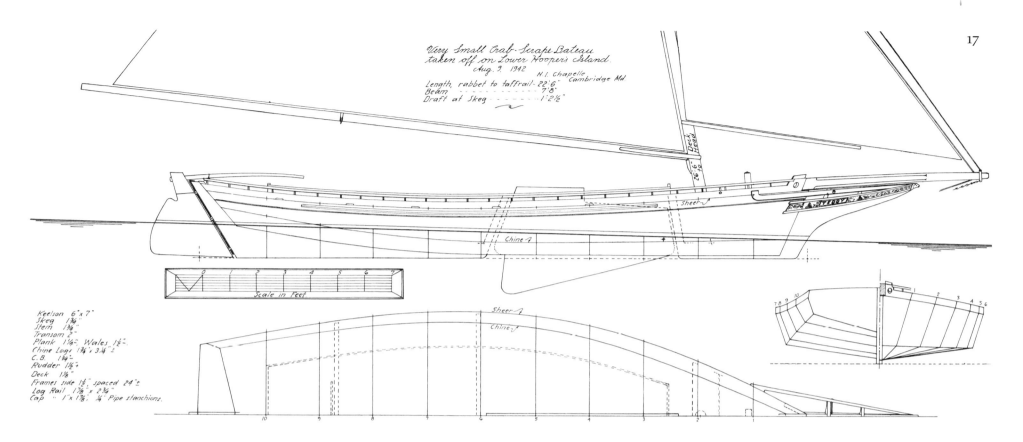

Very Small Crab-Scrape Bateau taken off on Lower Hooper's Island. Aug. 9, 1942 H.I. Chapelle Cambridge Md.
Length, rabbet to taffrail- 22'6"
Beam ——————— 7'8'
Draft at Skeg ———— 1'2½"

Scale in Feet

Keelson 6" x 7"
Skeg 1¾"
Stem 1¾"
Transom 2"
Plank 1¼"; Wales 1½".
Chine Logs 1¾"x 3¼"±
C.B. 1¾"
Rudder 1½"
Deck 1⅛"
Frames side 1½"; spaced 24"±
Log Rail 1⅞" x 2¾"
Cap 1"x 1⅞"; ¼" Pipe stanchions.

Chine

Sheer

Smith Island waterman and boatbuilder Lorenzo "Rooster" Somers Jr., born in 1914, recalled the scraping fleet of his youth. "Back there you scraped with a sail out here in the bow. I've seen white sails all on the [Tangier] Sound side there; they come from Crisfield, Fairmount, Deal's Island. I've seen a hundred out there. It's pretty in the spring of the year when they start. They limed their sails [to whiten them]. Boy, they took pride in it."[2]

When Chapelle studied crab-scraping boats in the early 1940s, he documented many of them, taking the lines of sailing scraping boats in various stages of abandonment and decay.[3] This was shortly after a period of transition in the design history of the vessel type. Chapelle noted that power had been permitted recently for crab scraping and predicted that

A small crabbing bateau as documented by Howard I. Chapelle at Lower Hoopers Island on August 19, 1942. Chapelle deemed her "one of the prettiest" he had seen and noted she was built by an expert carpenter, probably about 1900 in the vicinity of Deal Island ("Chesapeake Bay Crabbing Skiffs," pt. 2, *Yachting* [Oct. 1943], 58).

Laird's *Scotty Boy*, built by Lawrence Marsh at Rhodes Point in 1937. Her raked, V-shaped transom is reminiscent of the bateau form and begs for one of the shapely outboard rudders recorded by Chapelle. Many of the community's scraping boats built for power in the 1950s and 1960s retained the raked, V-shaped transom, but with the addition of powerful modern engines, they had to be equipped with "settling boards." These devices, also called "squatting boards" or "wing boards," are flat pieces of plywood that extend behind the stern, under water. They are usually braced by iron rods or wooden struts bolted to the transom. The settling board holds the stern up when the boat is underway, effectively preventing it from settling and dragging heavily in the water, as it is prone to do once the engine is installed and the vessel driven hard. Some crabbers use the settling board as a convenient platform for a custom-built live box. Its location behind the transom and slightly below the waterline is ideal for keeping the box flushed with oxygen-rich bay water, essential for keeping crabs alive. According to Larry Marsh, who

The oldest crab-scraping boat still in use at Smith Island, *Scotty Boy*, was built by Lawrence Marsh in 1937 at Rhodes Point. She has been used by David Laird of Ewell since 1958. Note the raked transom and settling board. The pail placed over the exhaust pipe is to keep out water. The low structure in the background is a crab-shedding shanty, a setup that has replaced the crab floats in the figure on page 40. The PVC pipe on the pier carries water to shedding tanks in the shanty.

the sailing crabber was "doomed to extinction."[4] Indeed, after World War II, many sailing scrapers were converted to power, necessitating modifications of the hull to accommodate the size and power of an engine.

In the scraping fleet at Smith Island today, it is possible to see remnants of the former hull shape designed for sail. The oldest scraping boat still in use is David

builds and installs them, the live box also helps stabilize and strengthen the settling board.

In the last several decades, builders of scraping boats have solved the squatting problem by "boxing," or squaring off the stern. This new design—simply called a box stern—has a wider beam aft, providing more work space than earlier designs. The box stern also creates more buoyancy aft, accomplishing the job of a settling board on a raked transom.

In the 1990s two types of engines are commonly used in Smith Island scraping boats. Many watermen use four-cylinder Cummins marine diesel engines, while others prefer six-cylinder Ford or Chevrolet automobile engines adapted for marine use. Both provide about 150 horsepower. Engine power is important for getting to and from the scraping grounds, as well as for towing the scrapes slowly through the grassy shallows.[5] True to the watermen's tradition of recycling gear and adapting miscellaneous objects for new purposes, several Smith Islanders use old beer kegs for fuel tanks aboard their vessels. The empty kegs are typically pur-

chased from mainland restaurants. Because of Smith Island's reputation as a bastion of conservative Methodism where the consumption of alcohol is officially discouraged, the appearance of the little keg resting prominently forward of the engine box, painted to match interior trim, is a striking anomaly.

At Smith Island in 1991–93, there were about forty-five vessels of the scraping boat design (although other boat types were used for scraping in a number of instances). About half of these boats were made of wood, while another six had older wooden hulls recently sheathed in fiberglass. The rest, most of them newer vessels, were fiberglass versions of the scraping boat design. Many of the wooden scraping boats were built locally in Ewell or Rhodes Point by Smith Islanders who had developed distinctive "models" for the basic scraping boat type. One such builder was Lawson "Capt. Lawse" Tyler (1882–1971), who built many a scraping boat and skiff at the waterfront in Ewell. In fact, one of his scraping boats, *Margaret H.*, was still in use by Capt. Edward Harrison in the early 1990s. Tyler passed along some

Smith Island boatbuilder Lawson Tyler, 1966.

of his boatbuilding know-how to a youngster named Lorenzo "Rooster" Somers Jr., who went on to build scraping boats, skiffs, and several large deadrise workboats as a sideline to being a waterman. One of the scraping boats Somers built, *Captain Brad*, is still owned and operated by Willard Laird, of Tylerton, whose only complaint is "she doesn't go very fast."

A third Ewell resident, Michael Harrison Sr., estimates he has built five crab-scraping boats and dozens of flat-bottomed skiffs in his lifetime. In 1989–90 he built a 28-foot scraping boat in his backyard in the traditional manner of

Capt. Edward Harrison in his crab-scraping boat, *Margaret H.*, built by Capt. Lawson Tyler. Harrison named the boat for one of his daughters.

Chesapeake workboat construction—without any drafted plans or half-hull models, but according to a design that existed in his mind's eye and all around him in the harbors.[6] Mike's father, Capt. Daniel Harrison, who has worked the water for sixty-some seasons, explained the informal nature of workboat building at Smith Island:

These pretty boats you see around here, a lot of them . . . the one I have now, my son built. He built four or five of them. Every bit of it, there was no blueprint; just by the— we used to call it rack of the eye. I don't know what that meant, but it's what we'd say. Rack of the eye. It means just using your own judgment. Boats were a lot harder to build than a house. Anybody can build a house where it's all square. But everything on a boat, everything on a boat is cut on an angle. It's harder to fit.

"Rooster" Somers likewise explained, "If you build a boat like the ones I built, you build them when you're in the bed of a night, when you lay there [thinking], 'What have I got to do next? What do I do next?' You're planning for the next day to go to work. . . . Especially when you don't build by blueprints. The only thing you have is your eyes to put lines on her."

About a dozen of Smith Island's wooden scraping boats were built by Leon Marsh at Rhodes Point. Marsh learned to build boats from his father, Lawrence Marsh (1901–63), who supplied Smith Islanders with boats and houses for decades. Leon Marsh has built scores of scraping boats, skiffs, box-stern workboats, and a few round-sterns since he built his first skiff more than forty years ago. About his first attempt to build a skiff, he remarked, "Most unusual thing is she was ugly because she was my first one. . . . She didn't have no sheer, we call it. Didn't know much about it. My dad was one . . . he'd tell you some things, but not everything. He'd let me do it the way I wanted so maybe I'd learn more. Learn by my mistakes."

By all accounts, Leon Marsh learned by his mistakes, and now the strong, sweeping sheer of his boats is one of the distinctive features of his design. A modest man, Leon revealed a hint of his pride in craftsmanship by admitting, "No, I never had a complaint. When I built 'em, I didn't aim to have no complaint. I never did have no comebacks. You know, like bringing 'em back and saying 'this is wrong and that's wrong.' Never did." Ewell resident Tim Marshall remarked, "I think a lot of the reason Leon's boats are pretty is because he builds 'em, you know, the way he would want his dream boat to be. That's

what I think, anyway. Somebody gets him to build a boat, they know what it's gonna be [like]."

Marsh's boats are known among Smith Islanders for their soundness and their distinctive lines. True to the Chesapeake workboat tradition, Marsh builds not from plans or half-hull models but from basic dimensions and construction techniques he learned from his father and subsequently developed through experience. As a craftsman steeped in the context of Smith Island's water business, his ideas about how boats should be built and how they should look are grounded in the occupational group's norms and values for working craft. Within the parameters of community norms for boat design, Leon's own sense of aesthetics, or "what looks good," also plays a role in the design of his crab-scraping boats. It accounts for such details as the strong, fair sheer line, varnished transom, and the stem's nearly plumb profile. He explained, "If it [the stem line] has a lot of rake to it, it don't look as good, not to my eye, they don't. Now the big boats like the school boat, . . . they look better with a [raked stem

Rhodes Point boatbuilder Leon Marsh.

line] but it's the lines of these boats, the straight bow with the lines looks better, you know."

Larry Marsh also commented on the look of his dad's boats: "And they have looks about them. People says they're pretty boats, and that means a lot, too. . . . Well, that was always my grandfather's and dad's way of doing it. If they're going to do something, they want it to look nice. They don't want to do something, they build it and say, 'Oh that's a ugly thing.

Left: The "right-side up" method of boat construction is favored by Virginia builder George M. Butler (right) in Reedville. Butler and boatyard worker Taylor Dabney fit the bottom planking on the deadrise workboat *Miss Betty.* The stem liner is clearly visible in the foreground. *Right:* "Upside-down" setup for boat construction at Rhodes Point, ca. 1980s. Note the keel, stem liner (foreground), transom, and side keelsons (chines).

I don't want that.' They figure if they build a pretty boat, that people would want it."

Like most builders of traditional wooden workboats in Maryland, Marsh starts building a boat upside-down, which has the advantage of allowing him to fit and fasten the bottom planks in a comfortable working position. The alternative, practiced by some builders in the Virginia boatyards around Reedville and Deltaville, requires the builder to nail planks overhead. The disadvantage for those who start upside-down comes *after* the bottom planking is finished, when the hull has to be turned over to commence side planking. Depending on the size of the boat, some builders can call on friends to help turn the hull with sheer muscle. For larger, heavier vessels, builders rig block-and-tackle from the rafters (or nearby trees, if the boat is being built out of doors) to turn the hull. At Smith Island, where boatbuilders typically work some distance from the nearest tree, friends and neighbors are enlisted for help in turning a hull.

The Crab-scraping Boat Darlene

In the mid-1970s, author William Warner spent a long summer day aboard *Little Doll*, a crab-scraping boat captained by Ewell waterman Morris Goodman Marsh. Warner's experience, recounted in his Pulitzer Prize–winning book, *Beautiful Swimmers*, includes a testimonial to the little boat's seaworthiness. Encountering rough seas en route to the scraping grounds, *Little Doll*'s captain assured his passenger that "these are good boats in a blow. Throw a lot of water, but ride all right." As the seas worsened Warner found, "True to her captain's word, the *Little Doll* rode nicely. She surfed down the steep seas, squatted a moment in the trough and then charged bravely up the backside of the next wave."[7]

Little Doll was built in the mid-1960s by Leon Marsh at Rhodes Point. Morris named the boat for his "little doll," his young daughter, Darlene. Although built for power, *Little Doll* retained the lines of the old sailing scrapers, with a beamy hull (10-foot beam on a 28-foot-long hull) and a raked transom, which required a

Smith Islanders help turn the 40-foot wooden hull of the workboat *Miss Jayne*, in 1975. The builder, Lorenzo "Rooster" Somers, organized the effort and remarked later, "When you're [turning a hull], you only want one person to call the shots."

settling board to compensate for the squatting effect brought on by the boat's engine. Morris Marsh worked out of *Little Doll* for another fifteen years or so, but then decided he needed more in a scraping boat. Compared to newer scraping boat models, *Little Doll* was small and slow, characteristics that, combined with her age, made working in rough weather less than an appealing prospect. "Used to

Morris Goodman Marsh in his scraping boat, *Little Doll*. Note the shape of the transom and the live box mounted on the settling board. Also note the awning stretched over the cockpit.

be," he said, "I dreaded those sou'westers" because they slowed him down. So when the time came to replace *Little Doll*, Morris went to Leon Marsh, knowing Leon would build him the new kind of scraping boat he desired.

Since building *Little Doll*, Leon had changed his scraping boat model. Most significantly, the new model abandoned the raked transom in favor of the box stern, which was simpler to build and bet-

ter suited to engine power. Leon Marsh's first box-stern scraping boat was *Jamie Lee*, built in 1984 for Ewell waterman Lee Tyler. Another four box-sterns for Smith Islanders followed, including *Miss Brenda*, in 1987, for Allen Marsh, Morris's son. Morris liked the roominess and stability of the box-stern design, but was especially impressed by the speed of the hull. In essence, he got tired of being left behind in *Little Doll* while his son sped ahead to and from the scraping grounds in *Miss Brenda*.

While Morris essentially wanted one of Leon's box-stern scraping boats, he thought a few minor changes to the hull dimensions would better suit his requirements. Having scraped crabs for thirty-odd summers, he knew exactly what he wanted in a workboat. The result is the scraping boat *Darlene*, named again for his daughter, and built by Leon Marsh in 1990.

Darlene's lines differ slightly from Leon's other box-stern scraping boats. She is a bit narrower of beam than *Miss Brenda*, and has 3 inches less freeboard from amidships aft. This extra low freeboard reduces the distance required for lifting the scrapes and suits Morris's preference for culling the catch sitting down. This feature also contributes to *Darlene*'s distinctive and dramatic sheer line, since her bow stem is the same height above the keel as other Marsh-built scraping boats, but sweeps 3 inches lower to the stern. *Darlene* fulfills Morris's other requirements as well: being wider at the stern than *Little Doll*, she provides a more comfortable working space. The high bow keeps her drier and the design of the hull, with its deep deadrise forward, keeps her "going fast at fourteen knots," twice the speed *Little Doll* could muster. As anticipated, *Darlene* allows Morris to work well in rough conditions. These modifications to the scraping boat hull form, while virtually undetectable to the outsider, make a world of difference to the man who works out of her. A finer-handling boat and a prettier one he's never had, Morris says, adding the ultimate testimonial: "and I wouldn't change one thing about her."

Building boats on a marshy, virtually treeless island has its own set of headaches, not the least of which is obtaining materials. *Darlene*'s keel, indeed, all her raw materials, had to be ordered through a lumber mill in Crisfield and imported to the island. Leon Marsh's brother Grayden hauled the materials from Crisfield to Rhodes Point aboard his deadrise workboat, *Dream Girl*. Transporting the keel—a huge timber of yellow pine—took special arrangements, with Grayden towing it behind his boat.[8] Upon arrival at the boatyard, Larry lifted the keel out of the water on the boatyard's Travelift. While it was still green, Leon shaped it, then allowed it to season in the open air for about three months. The keel continued drying out during the time the boat was under construction out of doors.[9]

Darlene was built by Leon, with a lot of help from Larry, under the Smith Island sky in the traditional "upside-down" fashion. One of the first steps in the process involved not building but digging, specifically, a hole about three feet deep to hold the stem liner (the structural member at the bow). The top of the untrimmed stem liner was placed in the hole, leaving approximately five feet above ground to

which other parts of the basic frame—keel, side keelsons (chines), and transom—were fastened. The purpose of setting up in this fashion is to keep the boat stable and at optimum working height for fastening the bottom planks. Like most Chesapeake Bay workboats, *Darlene* has a cross-planked bottom, with the planks running from the keel to the chine. While many builders of V-bottom craft cross-plank the bottom in herringbone fashion (with the bottom planks set at an angle to the keel), Leon prefers to set the planks "square," fitting the planks at right angles to the keel.[10] He begins planking at the stern and works forward, using random width (6, 8, or 10 inches wide), 1¼-inch-thick planks of yellow pine. Being nearly flat aft, the bottom planks near the stern fit easily into the rabbeted keel and can be fastened fairly efficiently.

Farther forward, where the shallow-deadrise bottom becomes a sharper V-shape and the chine flares outward from the stem liner, fitting the planks is more of a challenge. To fit properly at both the keel rabbet and chine, the forward planks have to incorporate a hard twist. In the past, Chesapeake builders simply formed this area—the forefoot—with hewn blocks.[11] More recently, boatbuilders have been steaming the planks to bend them into place, or shaping each plank by using a band saw. Others solve the problem by turning to fore-and-aft staving at this point in the hull construction. Leon Marsh, however, does not believe in steaming and bending planks because "moisture gets into them and the plank loses its shape." He doesn't believe in band saws either, having never owned one until quite recently, when he acquired a small model "that won't even cut hot butter." Finally, he doesn't think fore-and-aft staving is the answer either and has "never done it that way."

Instead, Leon fits the area farthest forward with thicker planking chopped out from 3 × 3s. This construction technique, which Leon learned from his father, was also practiced by boatbuilders in Ewell, including Lawson Tyler, "Rooster" Somers, and Michael Harrison Sr. Using a hatchet, Leon chops out each piece individually and fastens it in place with bronze nails. He then smooths the outside surface with a power planer, his one innovation on the technique of his father, who did the job with "a set of adze." This method results in a rolled chine at the bow, instead of a hard chine, which, according to Leon, often leaves a hollow look. Leon speaks of this construction method as forming "the deadwood in the deadrise," a phrase not often heard outside the world of Chesapeake watermen and old-time boatbuilders. He figures he generally uses about forty pieces of wood to form the deadwood in the deadrise and, sure enough, there are thirty-eight pieces of deadwood in *Darlene*'s forefoot. Leon estimates the process consumes about five days, more than twice the time the same job would take using a band saw or steam box. He said, "I take my time. I don't try to break any records. I take my time, try to do it right." Leon also believes his method makes for an extra strong bow and points out that he passed along the technique to Jerry Pruitt, one of Tangier Island's best boatbuilders, who continued the tradition until he acquired a band saw several years ago.

It was at this point in the construction of the boat—when the bottom planking was complete (including a coat of bottom paint)—that neighbors were summoned to help turn the hull. In the case of *Darlene*, about fifteen watermen, including Morris Goodman and his son Allen, came to help. First, they braced the hull on the inside for support, lest it collapse from its own weight midway through the process. Two men lifted her stem liner out of the hole, and then, joined by the others, they raised the boat on one side and lowered it carefully to the ground. The operation "went just like clockwork" according to Morris, who estimated the entire maneuver took two or three minutes.

Once she was right-side up, Leon fastened what he calls the "battens" inside the hull. The pine battens, known more widely as frames, run from the chine to the sheer clamp, under the deck edge. In *Darlene*, Leon used 3 × 3s placed 18 inches on center, that is, he marked off 18-inch intervals along the side keelson (chine), and placed the midpoint of a batten on each mark. (The battens provide a surface for fastening the side planks and serve to strengthen the hull.) With the battens in place, Leon then determined the boat's sheer line, the top edge of the hull, by the traditional "rack of eye" method. First, he clamped one end of a long, flexible strip of wood to the top of the stem liner and the other end to the stern. Next, he stepped back to "sight" the sheer and moved the wood strip up and down along the battens until it described the image of the sheer he pictured in his mind. He then clamped the strip of wood in place along the length of the hull. After measuring the points at which the wood strip crossed the battens, he duplicated the set-up on the opposite side of the vessel.

Ordinarily, a scraping boat has one or two side planks above the chine, but for *Darlene* the difficulties of island boat-building conspired to alter the norm. Had Leon been on the mainland, he might have noticed certain flaws in the pine or, as he said diplomatically, "I wouldn't have picked it out." But he did not get a good look at the wood until it had been ferried over; to reorder would have cost him both time and money. He decided to salvage strips of good wood from the yellow pine he was sent, and, instead of installing

planks in his usual manner, he strip-planked part of *Darlene*'s sides with 1¼ × 1¼ inch strips. Using 3½ inch bronze boat nails, Leon fastened the strips to each other, three nails between each batten. In addition, he nailed each strip to each batten, then glued the planks with Elmer's carpenter's glue, followed by "5200 hard rubber polyurethane marine adhesive sealant."

This was the first time Leon Marsh had

Darlene's hull, in the "upside-down" mode of hull construction practiced by Leon Marsh, April 1990. Note the cross-planked hull and squared-off, or "box," stern.

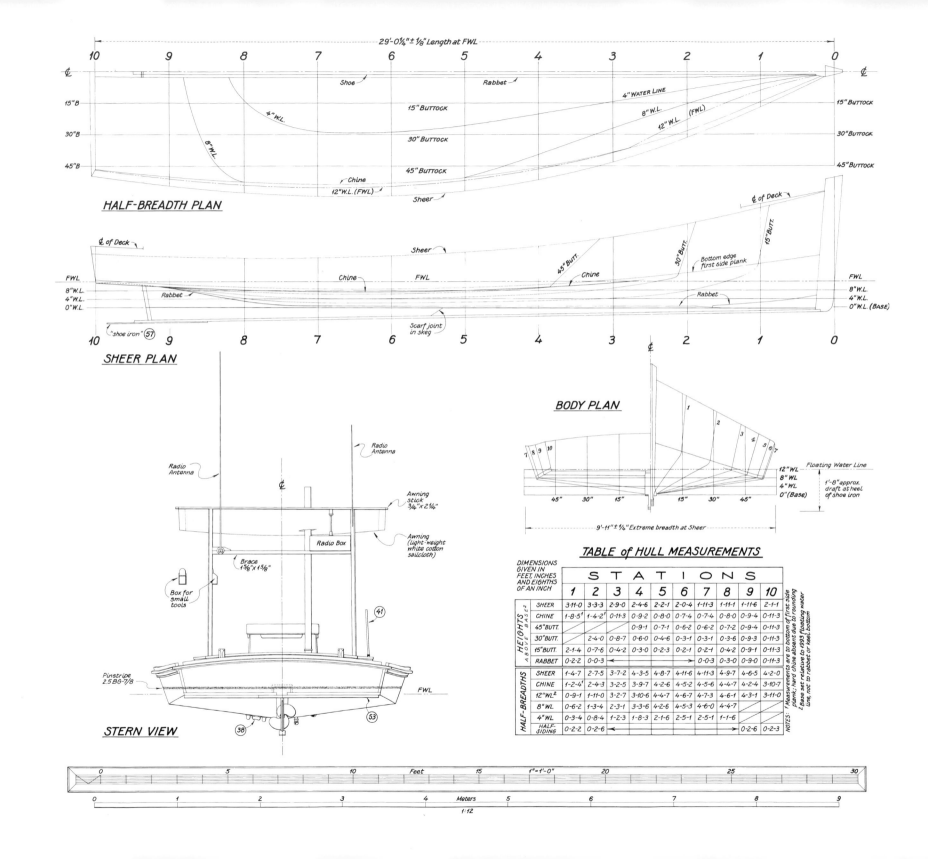

HALF-BREADTH PLAN

SHEER PLAN

BODY PLAN

STERN VIEW

29'-0¾"± ⅛" Length at FWL

9'-11"± ¼" Extreme breadth at Sheer

1'-8" approx. draft at heel of shoe iron

Floating Water Line

TABLE of HULL MEASUREMENTS

DIMENSIONS GIVEN IN FEET, INCHES AND EIGHTHS OF AN INCH

		STATIONS									
		1	**2**	**3**	**4**	**5**	**6**	**7**	**8**	**9**	**10**
HEIGHTS ABOVE BASE²	SHEER	3-11-0	3-3-3	2-9-0	2-4-6	2-2-1	2-0-4	1-11-3	1-11-1	1-11-6	2-1-1
	CHINE	1-8-5¹	1-4-2¹	0-11-3	0-9-2	0-8-0	0-7-4	0-7-4	0-8-0	0-9-4	0-11-3
	45"BUTT.			0-9-1	0-7-1	0-6-2	0-6-2	0-7-2	0-9-4	0-11-3
	30"BUTT.		2-4-0	0-8-7	0-6-0	0-4-6	0-3-1	0-3-1	0-3-6	0-9-3	0-11-3
	15"BUTT.	2-1-4	0-7-6	0-4-2	0-3-0	0-2-3	0-2-1	0-2-1	0-4-2	0-9-3	0-11-3
	RABBET	0-2-2	0-0-3	←				0-0-3	0-3-0	0-9-0	0-11-3
HALF-BREADTHS	SHEER	1-4-7	2-7-5	3-7-2	4-3-5	4-8-7	4-11-6	4-11-3	4-9-7	4-6-5	4-2-0
	CHINE	1-2-4¹	2-4-3	3-2-5	3-9-7	4-2-6	4-5-2	4-5-6	4-4-7	4-2-4	3-10-7
	12"WL²	0-9-1	1-11-0	3-2-7	3-10-6	4-4-7	4-6-7	4-7-3	4-6-1	4-3-1	3-11-0
	8"WL	0-6-2	1-3-4	2-3-1	3-3-6	4-2-6	4-5-3	4-6-0	4-4-7		
	4"WL	0-3-4	0-8-4	1-2-3	1-8-3	2-1-6	2-5-1	2-5-1	1-1-6		
	HALF-SIDING	0-2-2	0-2-6	←						0-2-6	0-2-3

NOTES: ¹ Measurements are to bottom of first side plank; hard chine absent due to rounding
² Base set relative to 1935 floating water line, not to rabbet or keel bottom

Radio Antenna

Awning stick ¾"x 2¼"

Awning (light-weight white cotton sailcloth)

Radio Box

Brace 1⅜"x 1⅜"

Box for small tools

Pinstripe 2.5 B6-7/8

"shoe iron" 57

Scarf joint in skeg

Bottom edge first side plank

0 5 10 Feet 15 1"=1'-0" 20 25 30

0 1 2 3 4 Meters 5 6 7 8 9

1:12

LINES

Lines lifted from starboard side of boat on October 6, 1993 at L. Marsh & Son Boatyard, Rhodes Point, Maryland by Richard K. Anderson, Jr. (documentation consultant) and Paula J. Johnson (Maritime History Specialist, National Museum of American History, Smithsonian Institution). Boat was set on blocks and a level line marked on keel. Field stations were chosen for shape and marked on keel from a plumb line (forward perpendicular) suspended from top of stem at cutwater. A scale was set square to keel and leveled to chalked level line on keel. Points on hull were plumbed to this scale for horizontal and vertical coordinates. Stations were plotted and faired to outside surface of hull, accuracy estimated to be ± ¼" scale athwartships, and ± 1½" scale for lean intersections fore and aft. Water lines were set parallel to the vessel's floating water line (FWL). Sheer is defined here as intersection between outer surfaces of hull and deck.

Buttocks and water lines are not usually drawn for deadrise boats with hard chines, but shape introduced by bow construction and stern rabbet could not be represented otherwise.

Lines were only taken of starboard side due to limited field time and assumption that vessel was sufficiently symmetrical to make portside measurements unnecessary. Later construction plan plots derived from laser level and water level measurements revealed (1) that the port side chine is about 1" higher than the starboard side with respect to a longitudinal central vertical plane; (2) that there is a slight twist in the sheer aft of midships, the port quarter being about 1" lower than the starboard; (3) that the port bow rais-

ings had greater flare than the starboard side. These characteristics were omitted from the construction plans, though supporting data are retained in the field notes.

COLORS

Colors evaluated by comparing unweathered paint samples to Munsell Color Standards in northern daylight (5600° K).

White: hull sides, guards, logs, washboards, collar boards, thwarts, awning sticks

Red (7.5 R -3/12): bends pinstripe, scrollwork around "DARLENE" bows; U.S. Yacht Marine Paint "Rooster Red"

Dark Red (10 R -3/6): boot and hull bottom, inboard sides of deadwood; Rappahannock Nº1 Interlux Red Hand Antifouling Paint, #50 Red (cuprous oxide 20 %)

Light green (5 BG -7.4/4): inboard bottom planks (except for deadwood), inboard keel, sister keelsons, engine box, fuel tank, built-in live box

Blue-green (2.5 BG -7/8): boot pinstripe (1"wide), U.S. Yacht Marine Paint "Green Spray"

Brown (5YR -3/6): collarboard and raisings caps, engine box top, snub-and-bitts, samson post; "Z-Spar #52, Teak"

Black: lettering and scrollwork for "DARLENE" in bows

Varnished transom: above boot, below guard, between white painted ends of side planks

Unfinished: inboard surfaces of side planks, side keelsons, battens, deck half-beams, deck beam supports, underside of washboard are oiled annually with pine oil, but never painted.

SCANTLINGS

Materials: unless otherwise noted, all wood is "Eastern Shore pine", commonly known as yellow pine.

Fastenings: all nails are 3½" heavy gauge bronze boat nails unless otherwise noted

Terminology: local terms are given below in quotations, with more generally used terms in parentheses

1) Keel, 9½" sided old growth "Eastern Shore pine"; keel is one piece from stem to transom. Keel was worked green, laid out 3 months, then seasoned in boat, according to builder.

2) "Skeg" (false keel) 2¼" sided, fastenings not determined

3) Scarf joint

4) Shoe, 1"x 2¼" white oak (Quercus alba), fastenings to skeg not determined

5) "Sister Keelson" (stringer) 2"x 2¾" nailed in

6) Scupper, 2" wide, 1" high

7) 10½" lap joint, secured by six 2½" bronze nails

8) "Side Keelson" (chine log) 1½"x 5½" beveled

9) Bottom Planking 1¼"x 7½" (average width) cross-planked square to keel, not in herringbone fashion common to skipjacks. Keel rabbet and chine caulked with "3M Polyurethane Marine Adhesive Sealant 5200"; each plank fastened to keel with 3 nails, to sister keelson with 1 nail, and to side keelson with 3 nails

10) "Deadwood", 3"x 3"s dubbed with hatchet to fit rabbet and chine, ends nailed in, outer hull surface power-planed and sanded fair.

11) Stem 5½"x 8" fastened to stem liner with lag screws driven from cutwater; fastening to keel undetermined

12) "Stem Liner" (apron) 5" sided

13) "Battens" (frames or ribs) 2⅜"x 2½" each fastened to side keelson with 4 nails

Opposite page: Lines of the crab-scraping boat *Darlene* as taken off on October 6, 1993, by Richard K. Anderson Jr. and the author. *Key to terminology continues on p. 31.*

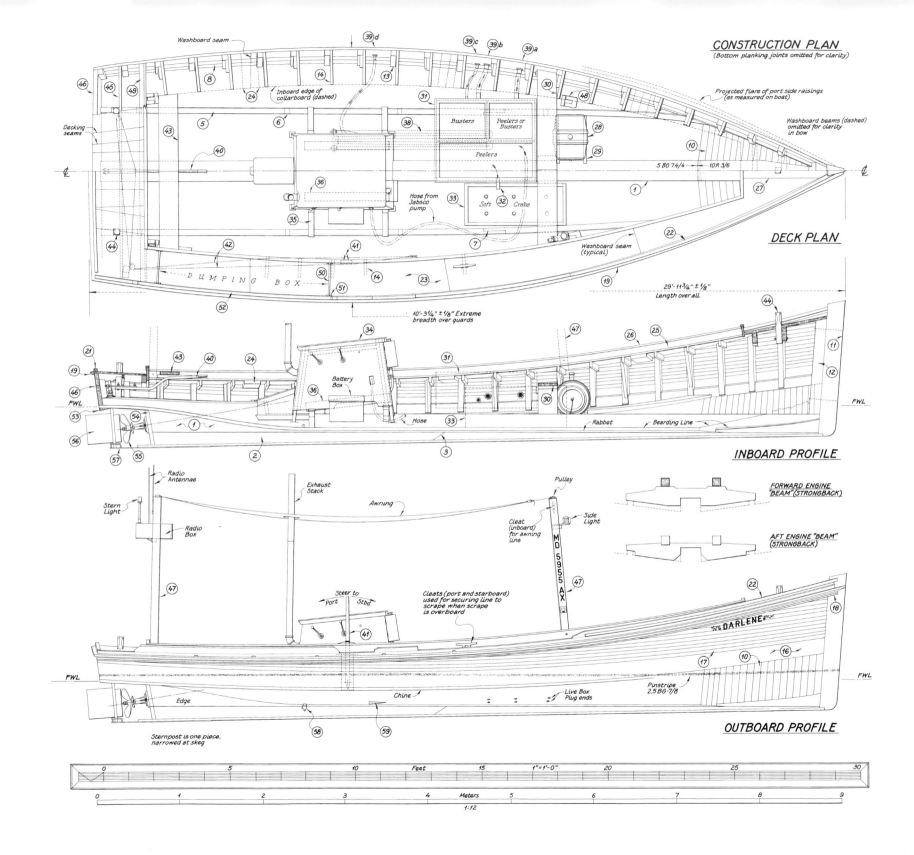

CONSTRUCTION PLAN
(Bottom planking joints omitted for clarity)

Washboard seam

Projected flare of port side raisings
(as measured on boat)

Washboard beams (dashed)
omitted for clarity
in bow

Inboard edge of
collarboard (dashed)

Decking
seams

Busters

Peelers or
Busters

Peelers

5 BO 7.4/4   10 R 3/6

Hose from
Jabsco
pump

Soft   Crabs

DECK PLAN

DUMPING BOX

Washboard seam
(typical)

52

29'-11¾" ± ⅛"
Length over all

10'-3¼" ± ⅛" Extreme
breadth over guards

Battery
Box

FWL

FWL

Hose

Rabbet

Bearding Line

INBOARD PROFILE

Radio
Antennae

Exhaust
Stack

Awning

Pulley

FORWARD ENGINE
"BEAM" (STRONGBACK)

Stern
Light

Cleat
(inboard)
for awning
line

Side
Light

AFT ENGINE "BEAM"
(STRONGBACK)

Radio
Box

Steer to
Port   Stbd

Cleats (port and starboard)
used for securing line to
scrape when scrape
is overboard

MD
5955
AX

DARLENE

FWL

FWL

Edge

Chine

Live Box
Plug ends

Pinstripe
2.5 B6-7/8

Sternpost is one piece,
narrowed at skeg

OUTBOARD PROFILE

0   5   10   Feet   15   1"=1'-0"   20   25   30

0   1   2   3   4   Meters   5   6   7   8   9

1:12

14) Half-beam, 1¼"x 2½"nailed one to forward side of each batten with three 3½"nails and to each support with three 2"nails

15) "Batten support"(hanging knee) 1½" sided, nailed to alternate battens with one nail at support toe

16) Side plank, 1¼"x 7½" fastened to each batten with 3 nails

17) Strip planking, 1¼"x 1¼" glued to side plank and other strip planks with "carpenters'glue", nailed to each batten with 1 nail, and to strips below with 3 nails in space between each batten.

18) Bends, 1"x 2½"; groove is ⅛"x ⅛", painted red (Munsell 7.5 R 3/12)

19) "Guard"(rub rail), 1⅝"x 1⅝"white oak, beveled; fastenings to bends and planking not determined

20) Nosing (or rub iron) ⅛" crowned x ¾" brass, fastened to guard and stem cutwater with nails every 8"

21) "Log"(toe rail), 1½"x 1½" white oak; fastenings to decking not determined

22) "Raisings" (toe rail); cap is 1¼"x 1½"painted brown (5YR 3/6); intermediate 1" sided painted white

23) "Washboard"(deck) ¾"thick 5-ply marine plywood nailed to each half beam with four 2" nails at bow, six midships; three nails into collarboard between each half-beam.

24) Butt blocks, 1½"x 7½" used to join washboard seams with 2"bronze nails

25) "Collarboard"(coaming) 1" x 3"fastened to washboard with three nails per space between each half beam

26) Cap 1"x 1½"fastened to collarboard with nails at 9"centers, heads countersunk and puttied

27) King Plank 2"x 7¼" (solid, not plywood)

28) Diesel fuel tank (stainless steel beer keg)

29) Fuel tank cradle 1½"x 1½" (tank unsecured to boat)

30) Forward Thwart, two pieces 1½"x 9¼"joined over keel

31) Removable Live Box, water supplied by hose from "3/4 Jabsco" pump belt-driven by engine

32) Overflow from Removable Live Box to Built-in Live Box

33) Built-in Live Box, made of 1½" sided lumber; 1⅛"ø holes in bottom planks (plugged with tapered wooden plugs when box is not in use)

34) Engine box, ½"marine plywood over 1½"x 1¾" framing; sides disassemble by removing top and unhooking hooks-and-eyes mounted in framing of box sides.

35) "Beams"(strongbacks) for engine bed 2¾"sided

36) Engine bed timbers, 4"x 4"

37) Engine(not measured):150 hp Cummins 4-cylinder Diesel

38) "Keel Cooler"or engine radiator (shown dashed) outside hull

39) Through-hull fittings, white nylon (plastic):
a & b: live box drain
c: live box stale water drain
d: automatic bilge pump

40) Tiller (1⅛"ø steel tubing)

41) Auxiliary "steering stick" (wooden)

42) ¼ø black nylon steering lines linking steering stick and tiller via pulleys as shown

43) Stern thwart, 1½"x 9½"

44) "Snub-and-Bitt"(bitt) 2¾"x 2¾", nailed to sister keelson, bolted to overhead deck beam

45) Deck beam, 1"x 1½", sawn to deck camber; beam ends nailed to battens

46) Transom, 2"sided white oak

47) "Awning sticks", 1½"x 3½" (commercial 2"x 4"), each secured to collarboard with 7/16"ø x 3½" NC bolt and nut. Starboard aft stick is notched below the radio box, each notch representing one week in the 1993 crabbing season.

48) Awning stick socket; "U"is 1⅛" thick plywood, end piece is ¾"x 1½" (commercial 1"x 2")

49) Aft collarboard/deck beam consists of a 2¼"x 3½" beam sawn to deck camber and sistered to 1"x 6" collarboard

50) "Dumping Box Ends":½"x 3"; crab scrapes were dumped in boxed-in areas of washboard astern where crabs were sorted; excess water drained through scuppers in the logs. Removable ends were secured by slots created by end brackets.

51) Dumping Box End Brackets: 1¼" wide strips of ½" 5-ply plywood fastened to dumping box sides (collarboard and log) with common steel nails.

52) Dumping Box side (outboard) 1½"x 2⅝", top edge capped with 1½"solid half-round black PVC (polyvinyl chloride) quard fastened to sides with 1¼"Nº 6 stainless steel screws

53) Planing wedge, 1¼"x 5½", nailed to hull bottom

54) False sternpost, 1¾"sided

55) Bronze wheel (propeller), 14"diameter x 22"pitch, mounted on 1³⁄₁₆"ø propeller shaft

56) Rudder, ¼"thick steel welded to 1¼"ø steel rudder post

57) "Shoe Iron"(skeg), ⅜"x 2¾"steel bolted to shoe; rudder post bearing welded from ½"steel

58) Water Bailer (bronze); inboard cap is removed to bail water when underway

59) Intake Strainer (PVC plastic) for Jabsco pump

Opposite page: Construction plan, deck plan, and inboard and outboard profiles of the crab-scraping boat *Darlene*. Note the live boxes, fuel tank (beer keg), dumping boxes, and strip-planked sides.

32

COLOR KEY
R = Red (7.5R 3/12)
B = Black
Background white
All letters black

NAME and PAINTED SCROLLWORK shown FULL SIZE
(traced full size from boat)

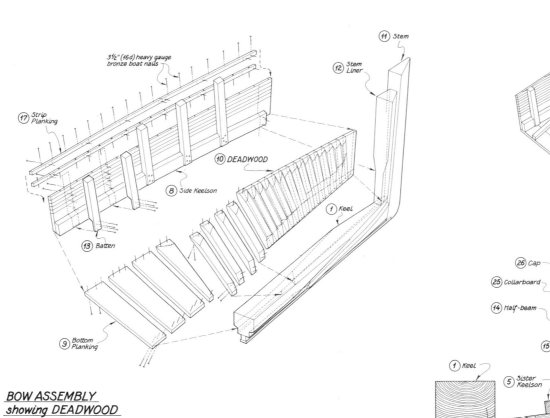

3½" (16d) heavy gauge
bronze boat nails

⑪ Stem

⑫ Stem
Liner

⑰ Strip
Planking

⑩ DEADWOOD

⑧ Side Keelson

① Keel

⑬ Batten

⑨ Bottom
Planking

BOW ASSEMBLY
showing DEADWOOD

Construction details of the scraping boat *Darlene*,

featuring the deadwood in the deadrise detail.

ASSEMBLED
BOW
(Bends, guard, washboard
and raisings omitted)

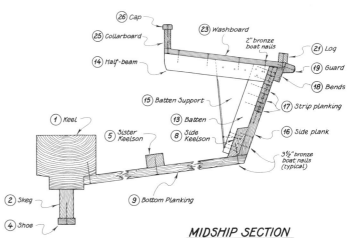

㉖ Cap

㉕ Collarboard

⑭ Half-beam

㉓ Washboard

2" bronze
boat nails

⑮ Batten Support

① Keel

⑤ Sister
Keelson

⑬ Batten

⑧ Side
Keelson

⑨ Bottom Planking

② Skeg

④ Shoe

㉑ Log

⑲ Guard

⑱ Bends

⑰ Strip planking

⑯ Side plank

3½" bronze
boat nails
(typical)

MIDSHIP SECTION

NOTE: Wood graining is for
illustrative purposes only;
graining was not field checked.

12"   0   1   Feet 3"=1'-0"   2   3   4

0   0.5   Meters 1:4   1.0   1.5

ever strip-planked a boat. (Most builders on the Chesapeake who strip-plank a hull do so on larger vessels to achieve flare in the bow, a shape more easily formed with many narrow planks than with a few wide ones.) But *Darlene*'s unflared bow is true to the traditional crab-scraping boat form. Leon estimates the strip-planking process took at least two days longer to accomplish than a typical side-planking job. Yet he says he would do it again, were he ever to build another boat: "I believe it makes for a stronger bow."

Darlene's washboards are plywood, and, according to Morris Goodman Marsh, they offer at least four advantages over the traditional wood-stripped or "sprung" decking. First, plywood is stiff but light and, therefore, saves on weight. The overall weight of the hull is reduced—an important quality for working in the extreme shallows of Tangier Sound. Second, plywood tends to hold paint better, no small matter when applied to the washboards, where the scrapes are emptied and the grassy contents culled. Third, plywood is easier to patch than wooden strips. Finally, plywood does

not soak up as much water as a wood-stripped deck, and, therefore, remains lighter.

The arrangement of gear is fairly standard among scraping boats in the Smith Island fleet, and a close look at *Darlene* provides a general understanding of the gear and work space required for crab scraping. The engine, a 150-horsepower Cummins four-cylinder marine diesel, is located just aft of amidships and is covered by a plywood engine box. Its fuel tank, a recycled beer keg (given to Morris by a chap who befriended him one oyster season near the Magothy River, north of Annapolis), rests forward in a custom-built cradle fastened to the keel and port stringer. The little keg holds about fifteen gallons of fuel, and, being made of stainless steel, "it'll last forever," said Morris.

Between the engine and its fuel tank are two live boxes, one built into the hull for holding soft crabs—the most valuable crabs—and keeping them alive. Bay water is allowed to fill the well through six holes, which have been drilled through the bottom planking. When the live well is not in use, the holes are filled with carved

wooden plugs. Another removable live box sits adjacent to the built-in well. Built by Morris himself, it has three compartments, each separated from the other by wire screening. Peelers are tossed into one section, while busters—those crabs in the process of shedding their shells—are more carefully housed in another, where they can complete the busting out process in relative calm. Traumatized busters can "hang up," or die, before completing their transformation into soft-crabhood. The third compartment serves as overflow housing for either peelers or busters. A pump, run off the main engine, keeps air flowing through the water in these live boxes.

The actual amount of work space on scraping boats is limited, with all the live boxes, bushel baskets, coolers, and other gear piled in for a day's work. Most of Morris's twelve-hour-long day of scraping is spent in the area beside or behind the engine box.[12] To steer, he manipulates the "steering stick," rigged adjacent to the engine box on the starboard side of the vessel. The steering stick is connected to the rudder by a series of lines and pulleys

Morris Goodman Marsh scraping for peelers and soft crabs aboard *Darlene*. The scrapes are overboard, and the towing line is visible from amidships aft. While the awning sticks are visible, the awning itself remains rolled atop the sticks in the stern.

how long he leaves the scrapes overboard. In muddy areas, where grasses tend to be thick, he generally runs the engine at 800–1,200 rpm, about 3 mph, for a lick lasting between five and seven minutes. On hard bottom, where there is less grass and the going is smoother, Morris runs the engine at 500–700 rpm, or about 1–1.5 mph. He generally leaves the scrapes overboard for about ten minutes when working on hard bottom, although, like any proficient crabber, he continually checks his scrapes to see if they are full and need to be pulled in earlier than expected.

After several minutes of towing, Morris begins hauling in a scrape, hand over hand, until it is next to the boat. He grabs the scrape by its apex, or eye, and lifts it aboard, a process William Warner aptly described as "a complex exercise of changing hands and body English which obviously required both strength and dexterity."[13] With the apex of the scrape resting on the opposite side of the boat from him, Morris stands inside its triangular frame and collects the net bag, emptying it on *Darlene*'s plywood wash-

in the stern. Because he runs two scrapes, port and starboard, Morris is required by law to empty them by hand; as mentioned earlier, use of a mechanical winch or hydraulic lift would force him to use only one scrape. The scrape lines are cleated to the port and starboard collarboards while "making a lick," the local expression for towing the scrape along the bottom. The type of bottom, muddy or hard, influences how fast Morris runs his boat, as well as

board. Before culling the contents, he returns the scrape to the water to begin another lick.

Morris, like a number of other Smith Island crabbers, has an ingenious dump-box arrangement that costs next to nothing, never wears out, and cannot be lost overboard. No crabber could ascertain when such "built-in" dumping boxes were first used, but they agreed the rig serves its purpose well. Slightly aft of amidships, the washboards are blocked off by thin pieces of wood called "ends." Two ends are used several feet apart on the starboard washboard and two on port. The ends fit into slots created by strips of wood nailed across from each other on the inside of the log rail and the outside of the collarboard. When ends are placed in the slots, the blocked-off washboard becomes a dumping box. The ends not only create this space for sorting the contents of the scrapes, but prevent the crabs from skittering out of the crabber's grasp. They also permit the watermen to keep a neat vessel, as the ends can be removed and the entire washboard cleaned. Many crabbers paint their ends to match the trim of their vessels; Morris has painted his teak brown to complement the color of *Darlene*'s log (toe rail).

Four vertical posts, two forward and two aft, support the awning Morris stretches over the deck to protect the crabs and himself from the hot summer sun. When not in use, the awning is kept rolled across the top of the two posts aft. Morris does not unroll the awning until the sun is high and the scrapes are overboard because it can easily rip when the boat is under full power, as it is en route to and from the crabbing grounds. The awning measures approximately 15 feet long and 8.5 feet wide. Brenda Marsh, Morris's wife, purchases the fabric—a lightweight, white cotton sail cloth—in Crisfield. She stitches the seams on her sewing machine before Morris staples furring strips in each end. He also cuts a hole in the middle of the awning to fit over the engine's exhaust pipe, and attaches two 4-foot lengths of crab-pot line to each of the forward corners. The lines feed through two small pulleys fastened atop the two forward awning sticks. When the awning is pulled taut through the pulleys, Morris fastens the ends of the line on metal cleats nailed to the interior surfaces of the forward awning sticks. Such an awning generally lasts about one season, unless the boat is caught in a gale, which can tear the awning to shreds in the twinkling of an eye. Morris has pondered trying something more permanent, like plywood, but he believes the boat just "wouldn't work right," as she moved through the air and water.

Morris employs his awning sticks for both storage and recordkeeping purposes. Should he need to make a quick repair to his scraping bag or cut something loose, he keeps a netting needle (filled with twine), a knife, and other small tools in a wooden holder mounted on the interior of the port awning stick in the stern. To keep track of how many weeks he has scraped in a season, Morris carves one notch at the end of each week in the starboard aft awning stick. When he changes the oil in his engine, he scratches the word *oil* next to the notch for that week. Thus, at a glance, Morris can tell exactly how many weeks he has scraped and when his engine is due for another oil change. At the end of the 1993 season, there were twenty-one notches and three oil changes indicated; a typical season runs twenty weeks. Perched midway between the aft awning sticks on a narrow shelf is a wooden box housing the VHF radio and other necessities—"fly spray, suntan lotion, sunglasses, and Rolaids."

Darlene's color scheme is fairly typical of scraping boats at Smith Island. Her hull is white except for the bottom, which is painted with red copper paint to help protect it from marine growth and worms, which can bore into the wood. The log rail and collarboard cap are teak brown and the bends are graced with a bright red enamel stripe. *Darlene*'s name and decorative motif at the bow—a squiggly arrow and leaf design painted freehand by Leon—are black and red enamel. Inside the vessel the deadwood in the deadrise is painted red, but the rest of the interior—keel, bottom planks, fuel tank, engine box, and built-in live box—are all sea-mist green. The exterior waterline is the same green, a shade Morris mixes himself of

"half a quart of screen-door green and a gallon of white paint." The lighter the green, the "easier it is on the eyes" when working. Various shades of green have long been associated with the trim on Eastern Shore workboats, and sea mist is the current favorite, supplanting the formerly popular pea green. When asked for a sample of the green currently on *Darlene*, Morris could not oblige, since the last thing he does after painting his boat is to mix together all the leftover paint to spread on the inside of his skiff. "Usually it's kind of brown," he said. There's not a speck of blue paint on *Darlene*, which is hardly surprising since many Chesapeake Bay watermen still follow the traditional taboo against blue paint on a workboat.[14]

Darlene's oak transom is perhaps the fanciest part of the boat, setting her apart from most others in the fleet. It is heavily and smoothly varnished, a touch that has become a distinctive feature of Leon's box-stern boats. Larry Marsh remarked, "People in this area of Tangier, down here in Virginia, they love Daddy's boats, my dad's boats, the way he built them. They

could pretty well—well, you can pick one of Dad's boats out of any of the rest of them because of the looks and they're nice boats. They're solid. They're built tough. . . . He always likes to trim the boat up in varnish work, have your varnished stern and your varnished bends around them, and painted up real slick, nice and pretty. And that's what people like."

Darlene is, quite likely, the last crab-scraping boat Leon Marsh will ever build. Poor health keeps him from heavy, sustained efforts, like building a new 30-foot wooden boat. In fact, while he was building *Darlene*, there were times when the going got rough. Morris recalled watching Leon struggle with a circular saw to trim the guard. The saw was "a-wiggling and a-wobbling," and Morris wondered what the guard would look like. The next day, when he returned to the boatyard, Leon was preparing to install the guard, and "when he put it up there, it looked like it had a-growed there, like it was part of it," recalled Morris, still impressed by the memory.

DEADRISE WORKBOATS

Crab-scraping boats are ill-suited to crab potting and oystering—the other major fisheries at Smith Island. These fisheries require a larger vessel with higher freeboard for safety, deeper draft for stability, more space for gear, a more powerful engine for traveling farther from home, and a cabin to serve as home away from home, when necessary. Most Smith Island watermen have such a vessel, called a "deadrise" (V-bottom), "bay-built," or just plain "workboat," in addition to their crab-scraping boats.

Deadrise workboats range in length from about 30 to 46 feet. Their beam is slightly less than one-third of their length, and they draw between three and four feet of water. Like the scraping boats, they are V-bottomed craft. Those built of local wood generally have a keel of yellow pine, a stem of white oak, with bottom and side planking also of yellow pine. Deadrise workboats are remarkably versatile, and can be rigged with hydraulic patent tongs for oystering, a crab-pot hauler, a soft-shell clam dredge, tongs for hard clamming, or a mast and boom for pulling up crab scrapes. Watermen who use their workboats for crab scraping say they perform reasonably well, but being of deeper draft than true scraping boats, the larger deadrise workboats cannot always work in the extreme shallows, where shedding crabs tend to hide.

Despite the basic similarities of Chesapeake deadrise workboats, there are a number of design and construction differences among models. Variations in design are most apparent in the degree of rake to the stem, the amount of sweep to

Waterman and boatbuilder Lorenzo "Rooster" Somers, in the process of building a 40-foot workboat in 1975. The house in the background is of a type once common at Smith Island. Mr. Somers' father, also named Lorenzo but called "Lora," built a number of such houses in Ewell.

the sheer, the flare or lack thereof in the bow, the amount of freeboard, the shape of the stern, and the finish of the transom. Each builder develops these and other, less visible, aspects of his model based on his preference for certain construction techniques as well as his sense of how a workboat ought to look and perform. Likewise, boat owners seek a model that meets their basic requirements for safety and size, as well as for performance, durability, and ease of maintenance. But for many the model must also suit their sense of what looks good in a workboat. Leon Marsh says his customers "want to know if [the boats] are well built, and they want a good-looking boat. If I'm gonna buy a boat, I want it to look good. I think anybody does. Although some people just don't care about that, just so they make that green stuff in 'em!"

How does a waterman go about finding the builder who will build him the boat he wants? How much room is there for negotiation about design between traditional builders and potential customers? Answers to such questions can best be provided by someone like Julian "Juke" Bradshaw Sr.,

of Tylerton, who shared his experience in acquiring his workboat *Miss Norma* in 1971:

I have a 41-foot box-stern, and I've had her twenty-one years. I had [her] built my own self. I've had three boats built in my life, the kind of boats that I wanted for me. The way you find a boat that suits you, you don't go and tell a man, "I want me a boat like this." What you do is look at the boats that's around, and when you see one that suits you, you go to that man that built her and tell him what you want. A lot of people says they're going to have one built like they want, but most [builders] won't even consider that. If you like a man's model or how he does his job, then he's the one to see about it, and tell him something about what you want.

Bradshaw described his initial conversation with Jerry Pruitt, of Tangier Island, Virginia, the man who eventually built *Miss Norma*:

You have to talk with him a little while and you have to have a little bit of money to start with. So we made a deal. I told him,

I said, "Jerry, I want you to build me a boat, and I want to tell you somehow about like I want her, but I don't want to change your model." And he said, "Well, you ain't got to worry about that, because if mine suits you, then I'll try my best to build you one like you want."

So I went down [to Tangier] that same evening, carried him down—I think he wanted one thousand dollars [for a down payment], and we got started on her. Well, right then I tried to tell him what I wanted other than changing his model, because they don't like to change their models. You know what I mean, what they'll look like. They pretty well know what they're going to look like, but I wanted the size of my cabin, I told him about that, and I told him how wide I wanted her, and really how long I wanted her. Anyway, he got started on her. I got him the money, so he said, "I'll start on her right next week, as soon as I can get the stuff." And he finished her that summer. It don't take him that long to build a boat. And back there then, see, he was just building boats, that's all he done, and he was a young man.

Well, he built a good, sturdy boat. . . . He made—I call it a pretty boat, you know. It

suited me. His models suited me then better than any. . . . Like I say, if you're going to have something built, you want it built [in a way] that suits you. You know what I mean. The looks of it, as far as going to a man that's a boatbuilder, that's the reason you see so many different shapes and models of boat. Their ideas is separate. I couldn't say to him, "Jerry, I want you to build me one of your boats, but I want the stern different or the bow different." The only thing you can have different is the cabin, maybe. You know what I mean. He could build a bigger cabin or a smaller one or whatever, but he don't like to do nothing to the hull of his boat.

Bradshaw's experience is fairly typical. Watermen are forever researching workboat options by carefully eyeing all other boats. Once they find a model they like, they talk to the owner to learn the basic facts: is she able [how does she perform], how has she held up, who built her? As Bradshaw points out, there is not much room for negotiation with a builder, because "he don't like to do nothing to the hull of his boat," although, as dis-

cussed earlier, Leon Marsh did make a few changes to his basic scraping boat model at the owner's request when building *Darlene*. In general, however, an owner's influence is only tolerated in details such as cabin design, color scheme, and details of the finish.

Experienced builders like "Rooster" Somers know the consequences of following someone else's suggestions while building a boat. He recalled:

There was a guy built a boat over on the Eastern Shore down below Crisfield and everybody come along—this was the first [boat] he built—they said, "I'd do it like this, I'd do it like that." Well, he kept changing and he kept changing. And, well, when he launched it over, he said, "That's everybody's boat." I don't think he even worked her. And then the next one he set up, they started coming again, and he said, "No. Stay away. This is going to be mine." And he done a much better job. Everybody's opinions weren't right on this boatbuilding.

When the customer is a member of the family, the builder faces special challenges

The round-stern *Mama Estelle* and a crab-scraping boat in Rhodes Point, 1965. The crab-shedding floats in the foreground are no longer seen at Smith Island. Crabbers now shed their peelers in specially built tanks ashore.

with unsolicited opinions, as Somers remembered:

We had an old guy, he was a Somers, in my family. I had to build the third or fourth scraping boat for myself. I would build them and sell them, I'd work them and sell them and to have something to do in the winter, I'd build a boat. He wanted me to do it right and he said down there one day, "You ain't

got the lines on her just right." Well, I hadn't finished with her, I said, "Well, do you want to put 'em on there?" He said, "No, I'm not building it."

Oh, he'd sit around, I had trestle benches . . . and that's where I dressed my bottom boards off so they'd fit snug. And he had a new pair of these "overhauls" we called 'em, blue jeans, and they were big enough for two of him. And I carried on with him a lot, he was in my family, and I said, "Now you're in my way again, George." He said, "I ain't in your way." I said, "Alright." So I was using twelve-penny square-cut nails, they were. And he was sitting down there and I was banging around him and I pulled them blue jeans off a little bit and drove that nail and fastened him to the bench. Well, when he got ready to get up, he took everything—benches and everything— with him. Well, it weren't in the Bible what he told me!

Like *Miss Norma*, the boat Jerry Pruitt built for "Juke" Bradshaw in 1971, the majority of wooden workboats used by Smith Islanders were not actually built there. For larger boats, in general, Smith

Islanders have looked to builders outside the community. The handful of boat-builders at Smith Island simply could not meet the demand for craft from all of the island's active watermen. In addition, watermen, by virtue of their mobility in pursuit of seafood resources, are generally familiar with boatbuilding establishments far beyond the confines of their own communities. By water, distances between Smith Island and various boatbuilders in Maryland and Virginia are not nearly as formidable as they are by land.

According to the 1991–93 survey, many of the wooden deadrise workboats (excluding crab-scraping boats and skiffs) at Smith Island were built in Virginia—at Tangier Island or in Deltaville or Reedville, on the mainland. These two mainland communities have long been associated with boatbuilding, due in part to their easy access to stands of good timber and mills to dress it out. Deltaville and Reedville are also ideally located on harbors deep enough for boatbuilding activity, yet still protected from the open bay. Further, these communities raised boatbuilders, men who grew up in the water business, learning the qualities of good boats and how to build them from their elders.[1] Such areas were well known to Smith Islanders. Not only did they share the same occupation with people in these mainland communities, they had easy access to them and their products by water.

Most of the older, Virginia-built workboats at Smith Island are of typical V-bottom, cross-planked construction, but with a distinctive elliptical, or round-stern, design. The round-stern should not be confused with the Hooper Island draketail model, popular on the bay in the 1920s and 1930s. The draketail was one of the earliest vessels to be built for power on the bay and had a remarkably narrow beam of about one-sixth its length. The distinctive stern, featuring a racy reverse rake that resembled the aft end of a duck, inspired the name "draketail."[2]

The round-stern workboat is most closely related to round-stern bugeyes and buyboats, larger craft used for oystering and hauling freight. For deadrise, engine-powered workboats, the round-stern design was the most popular model among bay watermen, including Smith Islanders, from the late 1940s to the mid-1970s.[3] Bobby Tyler, of Rhodes Point, whose *Mama Estelle* was built in 1957, said he went for the round-stern design "because that was the thing then." Likewise, he had her built by Hugh Norris, of Deltaville, "because that's where most of 'em [Smith Island watermen] were going" for their workboats at that time. There are now about a dozen round-sterns left in the Smith Island fleet, most of which were built in Deltaville or Reedville, Virginia.

The Round-stern Workboat Louise B.

Louise B. is one of Smith Island's remaining round-stern workboats. Owned by Jesse Brimer Jr., of Ewell, *Louise B.* was built for Brimer's father by George P. Butler at Reedville, Virginia, in 1966. Brimer named the boat for his wife, Louise, who still lives in Ewell. Jesse Brimer Sr. passed away in 1990.

The name Butler is practically synonymous with boatbuilding in Reedville, a small town located at the tip of Virginia's Northern Neck, the peninsula of land

Invoice for Tolson Brimer's round-stern work-boat, *Dottie Ann*, built by George P. Butler in 1957. This 38-foot workboat cost $1,350.

stretching between the Potomac and Rappahannock Rivers. Samuel Butler established a boatyard on Cockrell Creek, in Reedville, around 1906. At the time of his death, in 1933, his son George P. Butler (born 1911), was working with him, building and repairing workboats for watermen. George P. ran the boatyard and marine railway himself for many years and, in the early 1970s, he was joined by his son, George M. When the elder George died, in 1976, George M. Butler became the sole owner of the Reedville marine railway and boatyard.

By the mid-1960s, when he built *Louise B.*, George P. Butler had a well-established reputation for building sturdy, pretty vessels. Several Smith Islanders had already made the thirteen-mile voyage across the bay to Reedville to have Butler build them workboats of the round-stern design. In fact, the elder Brimer's nephew, Tolson, had placed an order with Butler for the round-stern *Dottie Ann*, in 1957. By 1966, when *Louise B.* was built, *Dottie Ann* had more than proven herself; George Butler's boats were a known quantity. According to Larry Marsh, who has worked on or inspected virtually all of Smith Island's existing wooden workboats at one time or another, *Dottie Ann* was "the toughest boat ever put on this earth." Larry recalled that Tolson Brimer had tried to get by with as little maintenance on his boat as possible, and because *Dottie Ann* was built sturdily and of such good material, Tolson rarely had cause to worry. One day, however, he went to Larry, concerned because his boat had a mysterious leak. Some mornings he found the boat with several inches of water in her and other mornings she was dry as a bone. Larry hauled the

boat so they could inspect her hull and they soon found the source of the problem: Tolson had worn a small hole through the bottom of the boat with the steering stick. Some nights the stick plugged the hole and other nights it did not, letting water seep into the hull. Larry patched the hole and has insisted ever since that, in terms of materials and construction, "*nobody's* boat has been as tough as Tolson's."

The distinctive round-sterns were built one of two ways, either out of chunks of wood (also called "logged" construction) or with vertical staves forming the curves.[4] Chunk construction is the older of the two techniques and the first round-sterns of George P. Butler were so built. According to Willard Norris, a boatbuilder in Deltaville, the chunks were shaped from large timbers. Five such chunks, laid horizontally, formed the bottom layer. "The second layer was set on top of that rim and lapped over the butts. Each piece was then bolted down." This brickwork-style building continued until the desired height of the stern was reached, at which point all of the layers were bolted together.[5]

The round-stern workboat *Louise B.*, freshly painted and rigged with oyster patent tongs, on the eve of her departure "up the bay" at the beginning of oyster season, 1992. Note the assemblage of makeshift anchors on the stern. Her owner, Jesse Brimer, prefers such weights over standard anchors because they allow the vessel to move slowly, in a controlled manner, over the oyster bed. In this way, he is continually tonging over new ground.

George P. Butler, builder of *Louise B.*, in his shop in Reedville, Virginia, ca. 1955.

stern *Mama Estelle:* "No [I haven't had any trouble with her stern], nothing that I didn't do to her myself. Running her up on the marsh, smashing up her skeg and sternpost. She'll last as long as I do, I expect."

One of George P. Butler's earliest chunk-built round-sterns was *Glenna Fay,* built in 1948. She was still working as a pound-net boat in 1993, hauling the harvest from several large, stationary trap nets set near the mouth of the Rappahannock River. *Glenna Fay,* 35.7 feet in length, has held up remarkably well throughout her long career, and only under extremely hazardous conditions did her chunks give way.[6]

Smith Island boatbuilder Leon Marsh, however, has a different opinion about the long-term integrity of the chunk-built round-stern. He reasoned: "Well, a big chunk has got some heart[wood] in it, it could have a lot of sap in it. And it'll rot quicker than . . . if you stave it out with white cedar. But a big chunk is going to rot." In support of his belief, he recalled the time when a waterman brought his round-stern workboat to the boatyard.

The chunk-built stern is widely believed to be extra sturdy. Elmer "Tank" Evans, of Ewell, had such a round-stern for many years and attested to her strength: "They're hard to build . . . . Lord, I don't know what it would take to tear one of them up. I don't think you could hardly tear one up." Bobby Tyler generally concurred and spoke candidly about the real source of his troubles with the round-

The man knew something wasn't right and wanted Leon to investigate. Once the boat was hauled, the problem became perfectly clear: the chunks were so rotten, they simply fell off. When Leon suggested scrapping the boat's round stern and fitting her out with a new box stern, the waterman agreed.

Leon Marsh's experience with round-stern construction parallels the opinions of Howard I. Chapelle, who noted, "At various times a number of round-stern bateaux have been built. Some have the stern staved vertically in about the same manner as that used in the New Haven sharpies. The majority, however, had the sterns built up bread-and-butter fashion. These sterns were hewn smooth inside as well as out and care was taken to keep the weight as low as possible. The bread-and-butter construction was prone to rot and staving undoubtedly was superior."[7]

George M. Butler, who represents the third generation of Butler boatbuilders in Reedville, has never built a round-stern workboat himself, but has seen a number of them "on the ways" in need of repair. "For the first ten or fifteen years they're

The chunk-built round stern of *Glenna Fay*, 1993. Note how the chunks are layered like brickwork, in contrast to the vertical staving in figure on p. 50.

fine," he said, but after that "they're hard to keep tight, they'll work loose. It's a lot of wood, there's a lot of waste. [You] have to re-pin, [put] tie bolt straps on, and they still tend to fall apart with time."

By the time George P. Butler was building *Dottie Ann* and *Louise B.*, he had abandoned the chunk-built method in favor of vertical staving. *Louise B.*'s staved stern is a masterpiece of construction,

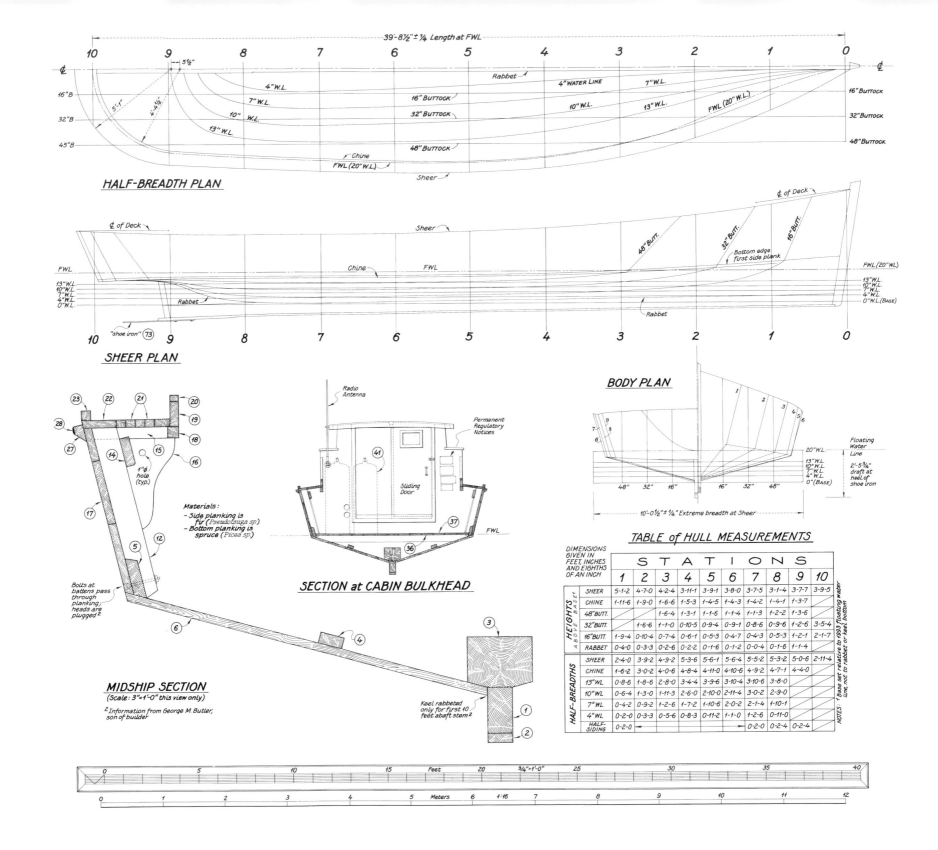

LINES

Lines lifted from starboard side of boat on September 8, 1993 at L. Marsh & Son Boatyard, Rhodes Point, Maryland by Richard K. Anderson, Jr. (documentation consultant) and Paula J. Johnson (Maritime History Specialist), National Museum of American History, Smithsonian Institution. Boat was set on blocks and a level line marked on the keel. Sections were chosen for shape and marked on keel from F.P. A scale was set square to keel and leveled to chalked level datum on keel. Points on hull were plumbed to scale for horizontal and vertical coordinates. Stations were plotted and faired to outside surface of hull, with corrections for list of boat on blocks. Lines accuracy estimated to be ±¼ scale inch athwartships, and ±1½ scale inch for lean intersections fore and aft. Water lines were set parallel to the vessel's floating water line (FWL). Sheer is defined here as intersection between outer surfaces of hull and deck.

Buttocks and water lines are not usually drawn for deadrise boats with hard chines, but hull shape introduced by bow construction and stern rabbet could not be represented otherwise.

Lines were only taken of starboard side due to limited field time and assumption that vessel was sufficiently symmetrical to make port-side measurements unnecessary. Later construction plan plots derived from laser level and water level measurements revealed that the sheer has about a 2" twist to starboard looking from the stern to the bow, but this may have been due to the way the boat rested on haul-out blocks. This characteristic was omitted from the lines and construction plans, though supporting data are retained in the field notes. A slight hog aft of Station 8 is shown in the drawings.

COLORS

Colors evaluated by comparing unweathered paint samples to Munsell Color Standards in northern daylight (5600°K).

White: hull sides, guards, logs, washboards, collar boards, cabin sides and roof, engine box

Dark Red (10R-3/6): boot and hull bottom; Rappahannock Nº 1 Interlux Red Hand Anti-fouling Paint, #50 Red (cuprous oxide 20%)

Light green (10 GY-8/4): inboard weather deck and inboard hull

Black: lettering for name on bows and stern

Varnished: cabin interior

Unfinished: welded aluminum mast, oyster tonging gear, engine exhaust muffler

SCANTLINGS

Materials: all wood is "Eastern Shore pine", i.e. yellow pine, unless otherwise noted.

Fastenings: at the time of documentation, bottom planking was being refastened with 3½" heavy gauge bronze boat nails; original fastenings could not be determined except as noted.

Terminology: local Smith Island terms are given below in quotations; in parentheses appear Virginia terms in single quotes, and more generally used terms without quotes.

1) Keel, 3¾" x 7½"
2) Shoe, 1½" x 3⅞"; fastenings to keel not determined
3) Keelson, single 8"x12" timber from stem liner to joint at shaft log; after which two 2¾" sided keelsons sister shaft log and horn timber
4) "Sister Keelson" ('Stringer') 1¾" x 3¾"
5) "Side Keelson" (chine log) 1¾" x 6½"
6) Bottom Planking 1¼" x 7½" (average) at stern, gradually diminishing to 4¾" width at bow; hull is cross-planked square to keel, not in herringbone fashion common to skipjacks; each plank fastened to keel with 3 nails, to sister keelson with 1 or 2 nails, to side keelson with 3 nails
7) Stem, 4¾" sided x 6" molded
8) "Stem Liner" ('Inner Stem', 'Stem Lining' or apron) 2½" sided; fastened to stem with ½"∅ steel bolts
9) Knee, 5" sided, drifted to keelson and stem with three ¾"∅ steel drifts
10) Samson Post, 3⅞" x 4¾"
11) King Plank, 2" x 8"
12) "Battens" (frames or ribs) 2¾" sided x 3¾" molded, each fastened to side keelson ('stringer') with one ⅜"∅ steel bolt
13) Butt Block, 1¾" x 7½"
14) Clamp, 1½" x 4½"
15) Half-beam, 2⅝" x 2⅝" nailed one to forward face of each batten

Opposite page: The lines of the round-stern workboat *Louise B.*, as taken off on September 8, 1993, by Richard K. Anderson Jr., and the author.

Key to terminology continues on p. 49.

Outboard profile and deck plan, with partial
construction plan, of the round-stern workboat
Louise B.

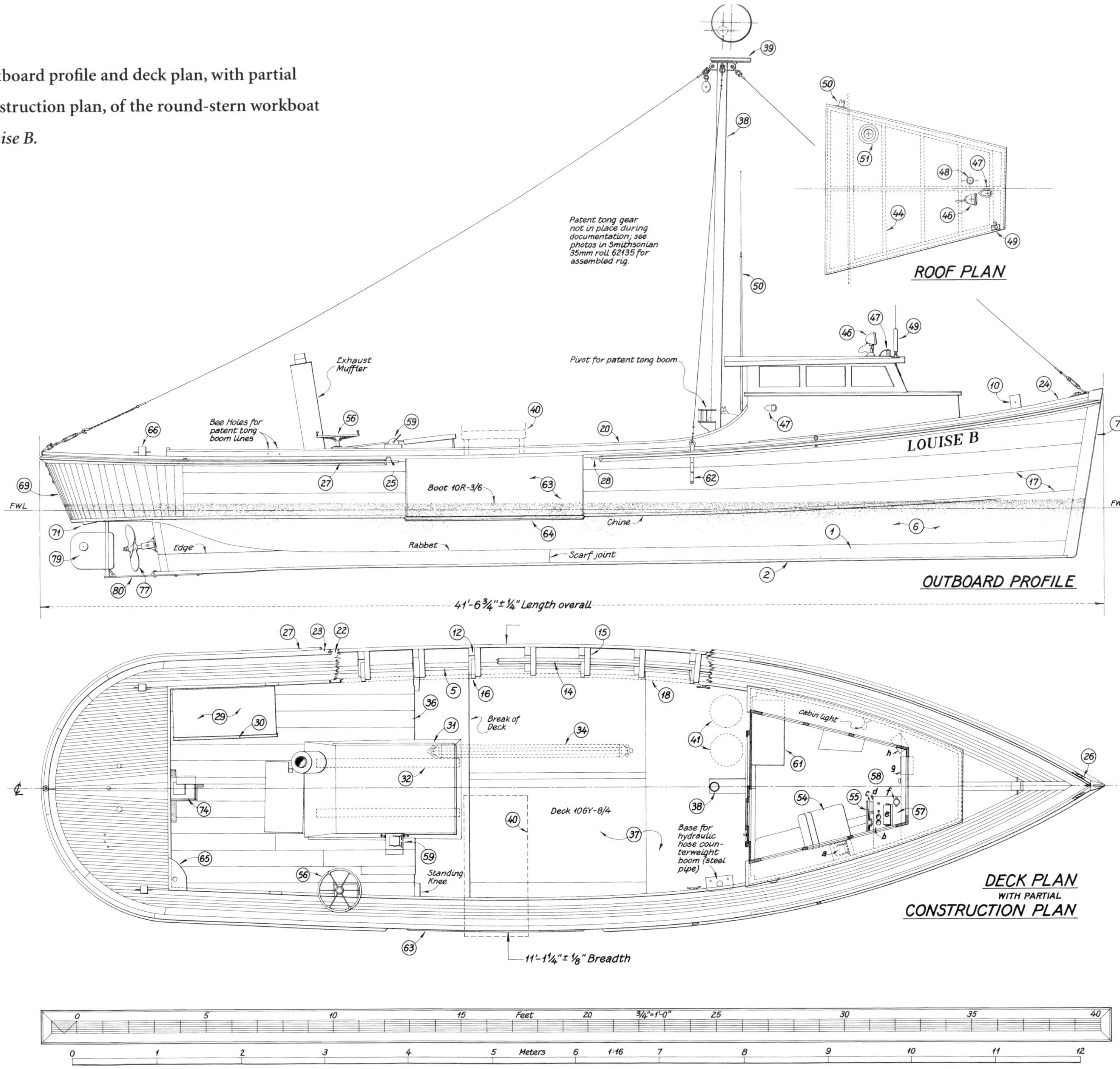

ROOF PLAN

Patent tong gear
not in place during
documentation; see
photos in Smithsonian
35mm roll 62135 for
assembled rig.

Exhaust
Muffler

Pivot for patent tong boom

Bee Holes for
patent tong
boom lines

LOUISE B

Boot 10R-3/6

Chine

FWL

FWL

Rabbet

Edge

Scarf joint

OUTBOARD PROFILE

41'-6¾" ± ¼" Length overall

Break of
Deck

cabin light

Deck 106Y-8/4

Base for
hydraulic
hose coun-
terweight
boom (steel
pipe)

Standing
Knee

DECK PLAN
WITH PARTIAL
CONSTRUCTION PLAN

11'-1¼" ± ⅛" Breadth

0   5   10   15   Feet   20   ¾"=1'-0"   25   30   35   40

0   1   2   3   4   5   Meters   6   1:16   7   8   9   10   11   12

16) "Batten support" (hang- ing knee) 1¾" sided, nailed to alternate bat- tens with three steel nails at support toe

17) Side planks, 1¼" sided, fastened to each batten with 3 nails

18) "Collarboard Beam" (carlin) 1¾" x 2¾"

19) "Collarboard" (coaming) 1½" x 4"

20) Cap, 1" x 1⅜" nailed to collarboard

21) "Washboard" (deck) 1¼" sided strips, each about 1½" wide, sprung to cover- ing board

22) Covering Board, 1¼" x 5⅜"

23) "Log" (toe rail) 1½" x 1½" midships, 1½" x 2⅜" around stern and at bows; fastenings to covering board not determined

24) "Raisings" (toe rail at bow); cap is 1⅜" sided

25) Scupper, 2" wide, 1" high

26) Cleat

27) "Guard" (rub rail), 1½" x 2¾"; fastenings to hull not determined

28) Nosing (or rub iron) 3/16" crowned x 1" alu- minum, fastened with steel nails on 6½" centers

29) Diesel fuel tank (steel) 60 gallon capacity; rests on ⅜" thick rubber mat

30) Fuel tank rail, 1½" x 1¾"

31) Engine Box, ¾" marine plywood over 1½" x 1½" framing; sides disassemble by removing top and unhook- ing hooks-and-eyes mount- ed in framing of sides.

32) Engine bed timbers, 3½" x 3½" reinforced by 3" x 3" x ¼" steel angle

33) Diesel Engine (not shown) is 6-cylinder 230 HP Detroit Diesel model 6-71

34) "Keel Cooler" or engine radiator (shown dashed) outside hull

35) "Beams" 1¾" x 5", (Deck Beams); spacing of some beams not verified aboard boat; some beams have been sistered with lumber of varying sizes

36) Old decking, 1" sided plank- ing (approx. 7½" width)

37) New decking, ⅜" plywood laid over old deck planking

38) Mast, 4½" ⌀ aluminum tube with welded lugs; hydrau- lically operated patent tonging gear is usually mounted on mast, but it was not in place Sept. 8, 1993; see Smithsonian photos 62135-17A, 23A

39) Television Antenna; TDP Electronics Model № 5MS750

40) Oyster culling board (steel); board size and location derived from Smithsonian photos 62135-17A, 23A

41) Propane tanks for cabin stove

42) Cabin Bulkhead ¾" x 2⅜" tongue-and-groove sheath- ing

43) Cabin Sides, 1½" sided planks

44) Cabin framing and roof beams, 1¾" sided x various widths

45) Cabin Roof, ¾" plywood

46) Spotlight

47) Running light

48) Old antenna base

49) Micrologic Loran antenna

50) VHF antenna mast

51) Stovepipe thimble

52) Stove base (stove not in place)

53) Locker

54) Seat Box and padded seat

55) Steering wheel (hydraulic steering system - no steering lines)

56) Auxiliary Steering Wheel

57) Control panel

58) Controls and instruments:
a: throttle and reverse levers
b: engine oil pressure and temperature gauges
c: CB (citizens' band) radio
d: fuse and switch panel
e: Micrologic ML-8000 Loran navigation system
f: Magnetic compass
g: Raytheon VHF radio- telephone
h: Furuno "depth finder" for locating oyster beds

59) Auxiliary throttle and reverse levers

60) Shelf for television

61) Shelf

62) Chainplate, ⅜" x 1⅝" brass; ¾" ⌀ eye section

63) "Board" (fender board), ¾" plywood, fastened where oyster tonging gear abrades hull; Smith- sonian photo 62135-17A shows segments of rubber automobile tires fastened over sheer for further protection.

64) Chine Guard, 1" x 2"

65) Block, 1½" sided

66) "Snub-and-bitt" (butt): 3½" x 3½", nailed to down chunks

67) Deck beam, 1" sided by 1½" molded, sawn to camber of deck

68) "Upside-down horn tim- ber" (horn timber) 4½" x 5", flanked by 2¾" sided keelsons through- bolted to horn timber with ⅝" ⌀ bolts

69) Round stern, built up of staving, 2" sided

70) "Down Chunks," 1¾" and 2¼" sided, bolted to- gether with ⅜" ⌀ steel bolts

71) Planing wedge, 1⅜" x 6⅝"

72) "Up Chunks" 1¾" sided

73) Stern blocking, 3" sided

74) Mast step, 2" sided; tonging was done from wooden mast stepped here until mid-1970s; moved to reduce hull stress

75) Shaft Log, 5" sided

76) Sternpost, 3½" x 5"

77) Bronze wheel (propeller), 4 blades, 22" diam. 20" pitch

78) Propeller shaft, 1½" ⌀

79) Rudder, ⅜" thick steel welded to 1¼" ⌀ steel rudder post; zinc once attached

80) "Shoe Iron" (skeg) ⅝" x 2½" steel, bolted to shoe

Inboard profile and construction details of the round-stern workboat *Louise B.*

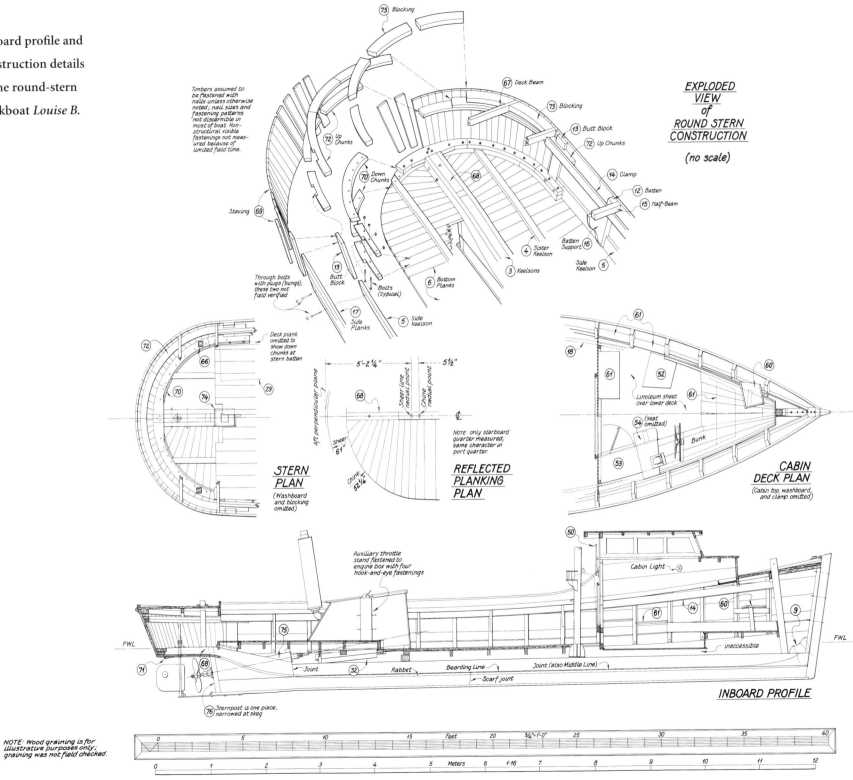

EXPLODED VIEW of ROUND STERN CONSTRUCTION (no scale)

Timbers assumed to be fastened with nails unless otherwise noted; nail sizes and fastening patterns not discernible in most of boat. Nonstructural visible fastenings not measured because of limited field time.

73 Blocking
67 Deck Beam
73 Blocking
13 Butt Block
72 Up Chunks
14 Clamp
12 Batten
15 Half-Beam
72 Up Chunks
70 Down Chunks
68
69 Staving
16 Batten Support
4 Sister Keelson
5 Side Keelson
3 Keelsons
6 Bottom Planks
Through bolts with plugs (bungs); these two not field verified
13 Butt Block
Bolts (typical)
17 Side Planks
5 Side Keelson

STERN PLAN
(Washboard and blocking omitted)
Deck plank omitted to show down chunks at stern batten
72
66
70
74
29

REFLECTED PLANKING PLAN
5'-2¼"
5½"
Aft perpendicular plane
68
Sheer Line radial point
Chine radial point
Sheer 61"
Chine 52¼"
NOTE: only starboard quarter measured; same character in port quarter.

CABIN DECK PLAN
(Cabin top, washboard, and clamp omitted)
18
61
61
52
61
60
Linoleum sheet over lower deck
54 (seat omitted)
Bunk
53

INBOARD PROFILE
Auxiliary throttle stand fastened to engine box with four hook-and-eye fastenings
50
Cabin Light
61
14
60
9
FWL
FWL
inaccessible
75
Joint
32
Rabbet
Bearding Line
Joint (also Middle Line)
Scarf joint
71
68
76 Sternpost is one piece, narrowed at skeg

NOTE: Wood graining is for illustrative purposes only; graining was not field checked.

0 5 10 15 Feet 20 ¾"=1'-0" 25 30 35 40
0 1 2 3 4 5 Meters 6 1:16 7 8 9 10 11 12

consisting of forty staves fit against upper and lower rims, confusingly referred to as "chunks" at Smith Island. *Louise B.*'s stern has a minimal rake of twenty degrees, typical of Butler's model and distinctive from other builders' designs. According to George M. Butler, builders in Deltaville typically put a thirty-degree rake on their round-stern workboats.

The *Louise B.*'s hull is cross-planked, with the spruce planks squared to the keel and fanned at the stern. She has two sister keelsons fastened inside the bottom planking, one on each side of the keel, to provide strength and stiffness in the bilge. *Louise B.* also has what Smith Island watermen call "an upside-down horn timber," referring to the distinctive reverse curve of the timber that connects the sternpost to the transom. This feature results in the boat having a concave bottom in the stern, which, according to one Virginia builder, "helps keep the stern down and makes the boat lie level in the water" when underway.[8]

What does the owner have to say about the round-stern design? Jesse Brimer Jr. extolled the virtues of his boat, *Louise B.*:

"I think [the round stern] works very good. See, you have to be at anchor, not exactly holding steady, but you want to drift very slow when you're oystering, and the round stern makes it easier to hold when the waves hit it, you know, as opposed to the box sterns are square and the waves hit that, gives it more force, shoves it faster. I think it works out pretty good, myself. A lot of people don't like it. It's not as modern as the new ones, but I like it."

Although few Smith Islanders fished pound nets, the round-stern style was also favored by pound-netters in the areas of Virginia—the Northern Neck and Middle Peninsula—where many of them were built. A pound-net fisherman's essential gear includes a small skiff, which is towed behind the larger boat and used for maneuvering in and out of the pound net. Many pound-netters find towing easier with a round-stern boat because the skiff "will glance off a round stern better than a square stern boat."[9]

Aside from her stern, *Louise B.* represents fairly typical Chesapeake workboat construction. Like most hard-chine boats, she has frames to strengthen the sides between the chine and sheer. She has no bottom frames, since her cross-planking provides sufficient sturdiness. *Louise B.* has three "beams" (also known as strongbacks), heavy timbers running from chine to chine that provide additional stiffening. One beam is located behind the cabin; the others strengthen the hull on both ends of the engine box, which houses a six-cylinder, 230-horsepower Detroit diesel 6-71 engine, only the second engine the boat has ever had. *Louise B.*'s sides are planked with wide fir planks running from stem to stern. Her washboards are "sprung," or strip-planked of 1½-inch wide, 1¼-inch-thick pine. Such deck construction represents a significant amount of effort by the builder and is rarely, if ever, used on workboats today.

For most of the year, *Louise B.* occupies a slip in Ewell's workboat basin, where she can be seen by the Brimers from their kitchen window. All summer long she sits idle while Jesse crabs out of his scraping boat, *Jessica Lynn*. But come October, waterman and workboat leave the rest of the family behind, and head to ports "up the bay" in search of oysters (*Crassostrea*

The Smith Island oystering fleet in its "home away from home" configuration, across the bay at Solomons, Maryland, 1984.

virginica). Because the oyster beds around Smith Island have been unproductive for years, most islanders, like Jesse Brimer, travel to other areas in the bay at the beginning of oyster season. Such leave-taking is nothing new for the community's oystermen; Smith Island skipjack captains and crews often left home to work for months at a time. For them, traveling back and forth under the skipjack's sail power every day was simply not possible.

In recent years the Smith Island patent-tongers have started the season in Rock Hall, a community located a substantial ninety miles up the bay. Typically, the islanders work out of such a port from Monday through Friday, returning to Crisfield by motor vehicle and then home, across the sound, by ferry Friday night. On Sunday the routine starts again with a drive back up the bay to their boats. This seasonal work migration pattern is the norm from October until Christmas, when many watermen bring their boats home for the holidays. It has become such a part of the community's rhythm that Janice Marshall, the multitalented "entertainment director" for various Smith Is-

land celebrations, has composed lyrics about it. Sung to the tune of Willie Nelson's "On the Road Again," her verses put a humorous spin on what the work pattern means from both the men's and women's perspectives:

(Men)
Up the bay again
I just can't wait to get up the bay again
The life I love is tonging oysters with my
*   friends*
I can't wait to get up the bay again.

Up the bay again
Eating places [restaurants] where I've never
*   been*
Tonging rocks [oyster beds] that I may never
*   see again*
I can't wait to get up the bay again.

Up the bay again
Every Sunday we ride up the highway
We're the best of friends
Wishing that the market goes up
Our way and our way.

(Women)
Up the bay again
I just can't wait 'til he's up the bay again

The life I love is going shopping with my
*   friends*
I can't wait 'til he's up the bay again.

He's up the bay again
I'm spending money places I have never
*   been*
Shopping centers I may never see again
I can't wait 'til he's up the bay again.

Up the bay again
Every Sunday he goes up the highway
*   with all his friends*
He can stay as long as he sends
His money my way, yeah my way.[10]

For oystering up the bay, *Louise B.* is rigged with hydraulic patent tongs—heavy toothed iron jaws, which open and close in a scissorlike fashion. The tongs are rigged to a length of sturdy line that operates off a winch mounted to a mast and boom aft of the bulkhead. Like most patent-tongers of the past thirty years, Jesse operates the tongs by depressing hydraulic foot pedals mounted on the deck. He has installed two foot pedals: one for dropping and winding in the tongs, and the other for opening and closing them.[11]

Julian "Juke" Bradshaw Sr. with his box-stern deadrise workboat at the L. Marsh & Son Boat Yard in Rhodes Point, 1993.

legal oysters (those that are at least three inches in length), which are tossed forward in a pile on the deck, and "throwbacks," the empty shells, mud, and other detritus brought up by the tongs.[12] The throwbacks are shoved overboard as the next tongful of oyster bottom emerges. While tonging, Jesse anchors off the stern, using one of his many makeshift anchors. In the manner of waste not / want not, an occupational value so central to watermen, his anchors include discarded engine blocks and crankshafts. Such anchors are favored over conventional types not only for their economy, but also for the controlled amount of drag that allows a boat to move slowly about the oyster bed, away from the spot that has just been worked.

Thus, after sending the tongs overboard with one pedal, he closes them — taking a bite out of the oyster bed below — by stepping on the other. By jamming his foot on the first pedal, he brings the filled tongs topsides; a step on the other pedal opens them over the culling board, which sits athwartships. As Jesse drops the tongs back overboard for another "dip," he sorts the contents of the culling board into

Because Smith Island oystermen work so far away from home, their boats become much more than just a work space during oyster season. Boats like *Louise B.* are transformed into a home away from home, and the vessel's cabin takes on a whole new ambiance. Some watermen have rigged their cabins with comfortable bedding, portable heater, microwave oven, and television, while others make do with fewer amenities. *Louise B.*'s cabin is somewhere in between, with curtains for privacy, television for entertainment, propane stoves for heating and limited cooking, and a pillow and blankets for a fair night's sleep. Jesse explained:

It's really not too bad to be away from home in the early fall. Warm weather, you know. If there's going to be any money made oystering, you make it in the fall. That's the start of the season and you have decent weather. We have television on our boats. We mostly eat in restaurants, which gets boring after a while. Like I say, if you have maybe twenty-five people from your home, that helps out a lot, you know. You don't feel like you're left out altogether of your home life. You can talk and somebody's always calling home to see if there's any problems, you know. We call maybe once or twice a week. It gets old, and the colder the weather gets after Christmas, it gets boring. Everybody wants to get home.

The majority of deadrise workboats at Smith Island, as elsewhere on the bay, were constructed more recently than the round-stern models. Like new crab-scraping boats, the newer bay-builts have squared or box sterns. Easier to build and maintain, the box stern also provides more room across the transom for working or for hauling gear. Julian "Juke" Bradshaw Sr. explained part of the appeal of box-stern boats: "What I liked about her [*Miss Norma*], she was a box-stern. Back there not many years ago, you couldn't even buy a box-stern. They were all round-stern boats, and this type boat [box-stern] would go some if you had power enough, put enough power in her. She'd come out on it just like a yacht would, and that was one of the reasons we liked them."

It is quite unlikely that any new wooden round-stern workboats will be built in the Chesapeake region. The installation of the stern is difficult and time consuming, and many watermen now favor the more updated look of the box-stern. Several of Smith Island's round-sterns, like Jennings Evans's old *Rogatorro*,[13] have wound up in the marsh, the final resting place for wooden workboats that have outlived their usefulness.

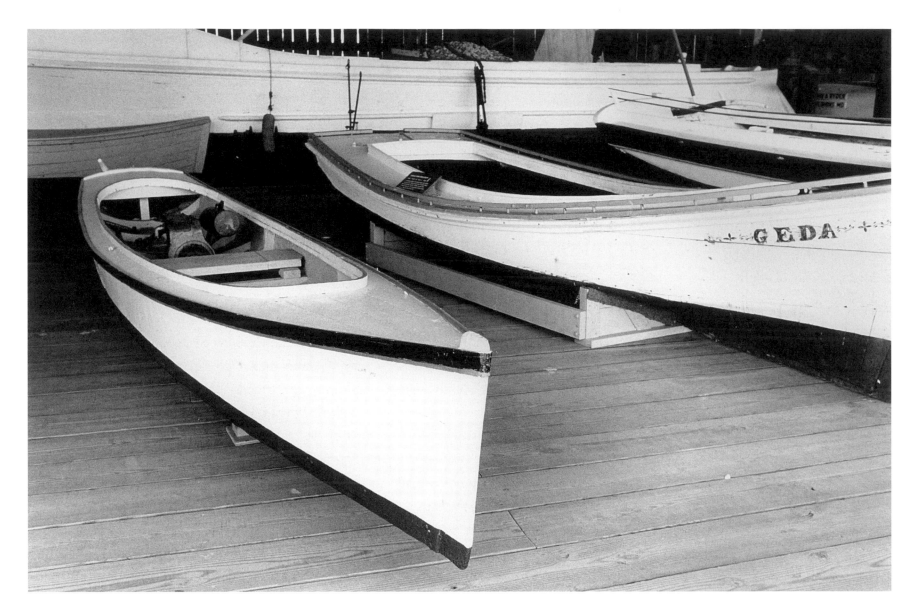

Two Smith Island–built vessels have found a home in the collections of the Calvert Marine Museum in Solomons, Maryland. *Left*, the fore-and-aft planked skiff attributed to Capt. Lawson Tyler; *right*, *Geda*, a small crab-scraping boat built by Leon Marsh in the 1950s.

SKIFFS

She was built at Smith Island, Maryland; this small island village has built a large number of skiffs of varying models and rigs and the builders have quite a reputation for producing fast boats.

Howard I. Chapelle, "Chesapeake Bay Crabbing Skiffs"

Skiffs comprise the third category of workboat at Smith Island, a grouping that includes any small, open boat, usually 18 feet in length or shorter. Skiffs are typically powered by an outboard motor mounted on the transom. At Smith Island, skiffs are the most numerous of any boat type—136 were counted in the 1991–93 survey—and are the most widely and frequently used.[1] Islanders use skiffs the way mainlanders might use bicycles or automobiles: for basic transportation, to run errands, or, as Larry Marsh said, "to sport around in on weekends." Such sport includes running the "guts," the narrow, shallow passages that wind and loop through the vast Smith Island marshes. Skiffs are also used by Smith Islanders for certain types of work, such as netting soft crabs, running a trotline for hard crabs,

catching fish for the table, hunting ducks, or hand-tonging up a few oysters.

The oldest skiffs at Smith Island are made of wood and, for the most part, were built locally. Some watermen built their own simple skiffs while others relied on the craftsmanship of various builders already mentioned—the late "Capt. Lawse" Tyler and Lawrence Marsh, "Rooster" Somers, Leon Marsh, and Mike Harrison Sr. Among them, these boatbuilders constructed hundreds of flat-bottomed or shallow, V-bottom wooden skiffs for generations of islanders. In conversations with people at Smith Island, "Captain Lawse" was often named as a prolific builder of boats, especially skiffs, at Ewell. Attempts to locate one of his skiffs still in use at Smith Island were unsuccessful, yet one attributed to him

A Smith Island "speed boat" of the type built by Capt. Lawson Tyler.

tive feature is her fore-and-aft bottom planking, a radical departure from the cross-planked construction of most bay craft, including virtually all extant wooden skiffs at Smith Island.

Captain Lawse's speed boat raises a number of questions concerning its place in the boat design heritage at Smith Island. How does fore-and-aft bottom planking fit into the repertory of V-bottom boatbuilding at Smith Island? Where did it come from and how widespread was this method of bottom construction? Was Captain Lawse's model idiosyncratic, or were other builders at the time planking their small, V-bottom hulls in this manner? Considering the nature of vernacular, or folk, boatbuilding, one would expect to find evidence of other fore-and-aft planked hulls from Smith Island. Vernacular boatbuilding, like other expressive forms in traditional communities, is essentially conservative. While certain aspects of boat design and construction may vary with a builder's personal tastes and skills, they do so within the parameters of community norms, or "localized notions of correctness."[3] In other words,

has been preserved in the collections of the Calvert Marine Museum in Solomons, Maryland.[2] According to the museum's files, this shallow, deadrise skiff was built "in the early 1900s" and is 18 feet, 8 inches long, with a strikingly narrow beam of 3 feet, 8 inches, and 1 foot, 5 inches depth. Called a "speed boat" by Smith Islanders, she was built to be engine powered, and would have been among the first generation or two of skiffs built for inboard power at Smith Island. Her most distinc-

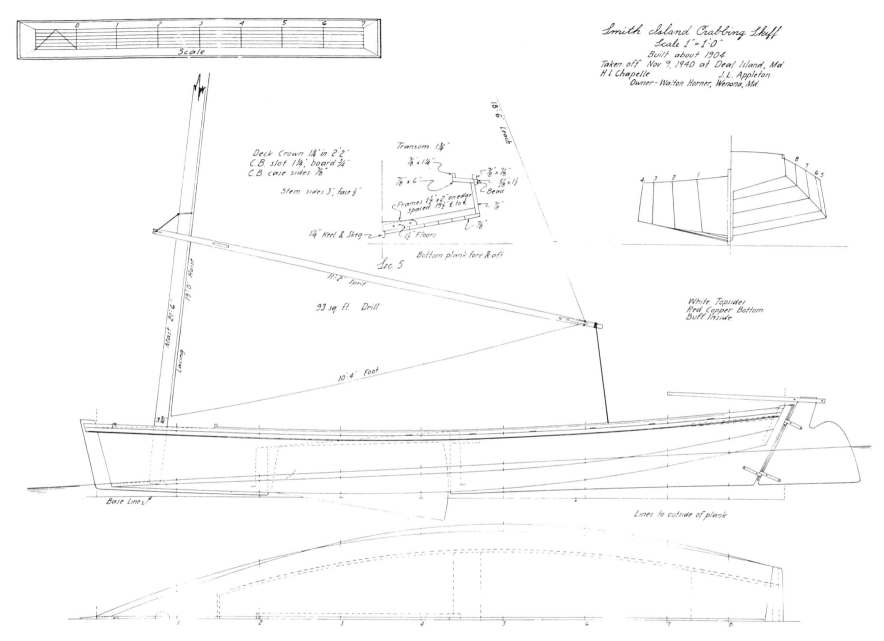

Smith Island Crabbing Skiff
Scale 1"=1'0"
Built about 1904
Taken off Nov 9, 1940 at Deal Island, Md.
H.I. Chapelle   J.L. Appleton
Owner - Walton Horner, Wenona, Md.

Deck Crown 1½" in 2'2"
C.B. slot 1¼, board ¾
C.B. case sides ⅞"

Stem sides 3", face ⅝"

Transom 1¾
⅞ x 1¼
⅞ x 6
⅞" x ⅞
5⁄16 x 1½
Bead
Frames 1½" x 2" on edge
spaced 19½ ℄ to ℄
1¼" Keel & Skeg
1½ Floors
⅞
Sec. 5
Bottom plank fore & aft

White Topsides
Red Copper Bottom
Buff Inside.

18'6" Leach
11'2" Sprit
93 sq. ft.   Drill
10'4" Foot
Mast 2'6"
19'0 Hoist
Lacing
3¾

Base Line

Lines to outside of plank

A fore-and-aft planked sailing skiff documented by Howard I. Chapelle in 1940 at Deal Island, Maryland. The vessel had been built ca. 1904 at Smith Island.

SKIFFS

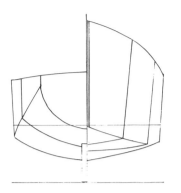

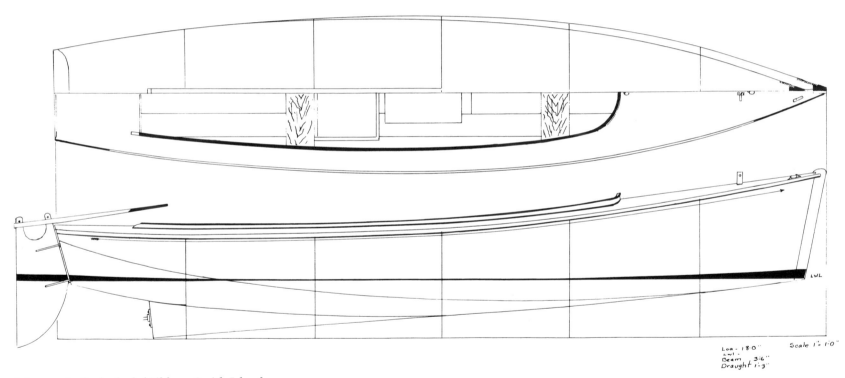

Loa - 18'-0"
Lwl -
Beam 3'-6"
Draught 1'-3"

Scale 1" = 1'-0"

A fore-and-aft planked skiff from Smith Island
documented by the Historic American Merchant
Marine Survey in 1937.

outlandish boat designs or idiosyncratic construction techniques are not likely to flourish in a community of traditional watermen.

From available evidence, it appears that, indeed, the fore-and-aft bottom planking of the Captain Lawse speed boat is not so unusual, taken in the context of its specific locality and time. Two very similar vessels—power skiffs believed to have been built in the vicinity of Smith Island in the early 1920s—have been preserved in the small-craft collections of the Chesapeake Bay Maritime Museum in St. Michaels, Maryland. Both have fore-and-aft bottom planking and other details of construction reminiscent of the skiff at Calvert Marine Museum.[4] Evidence of the skiff's likely predecessor is provided by Howard I. Chapelle, who, in 1940, recorded what he deemed a "highly unorthodox V-bottom model," a 17-foot fore-and-aft planked sailing skiff built at Smith Island circa 1904. In the wider context of Chesapeake Bay boatbuilding, this skiff *was* unusual, being "one of the two Bay types of dead-rise small boat that is fore-and-aft planked on the bottom." The result of this con-struction detail, according to Chapelle, was that the fore-and-aft planked skiff had "a much fairer [smoother] bottom" than was found on the typical cross-planked boats. That this feature allowed the skiff to reach high speeds gave her "a good reputation with the watermen."[5]

Such clues indicate that fore-and-aft bottom planking for small sailing and early power skiffs was an accepted and practiced construction method employed at Smith Island early in this century. Lawson Tyler, born in 1882, would certainly have been aware of such techniques, and it is likely he practiced them. "Rooster" Somers, who acquired some of his boatbuilding know-how from Tyler, confirmed that his mentor planked his speed boats in the fore-and-aft fashion. Somers himself, however, practiced only the typical Chesapeake Bay cross-planking method in his long boatbuilding career. How widespread fore-and-aft bottom planking was outside the community is not known, although it was certainly in the repertory of techniques used by boatbuilders along the lower Potomac. There they were building Potomac River dory boats, the other type

A skiff built by Haynie Marshall in Tylerton, ca. 1974, owned by Ernest Kitching of Ewell. A culling board rests athwartships.

A Smith Islander netting crabs from the foredeck
of his wooden skiff.

of fore-and-aft planked, small deadrise boat alluded to by Chapelle.[6]

Rhodes Point boatbuilder Leon Marsh has built a few skiffs in recent years, including one in 1994 intended for his son, Larry. Like the cobbler's children who go without shoes, the boatbuilder at Smith Island often finds himself skiffless. Leon Marsh explained, "When I started them [building a boat], setting them up, they always come and ask for it, speak for it. I never had no advertisements whatsoever on a boat. I could never keep a skiff of my own. I'd build it and somebody'd offer a price for it and I'd take it. I'd have no skiff. I've had new outboards [motors] on skiffs. They've bought the skiff and I've taken the new outboard off and brought her in." Sure enough, the skiff meant for Larry Marsh wound up in the hands of a man from the Eastern Shore of Virginia, who made Leon an offer he could not refuse.

A corollary to this phenomenon was mentioned by "Rooster" Somers's wife, Eileen. She remembered, "It was one guy said, 'If you ever want to sell your boats, say you built it for your son and then they

know you've done the best you can.'" Her husband added, "That was Capt. Lawse's motto. When . . . nobody wanted one built, he'd start building one, these speed boats. And they'd say, 'Capt. Lawse? Who's that for?' And his boy was named Norman and he talked real fast and [he would] say, 'That's Norman's.' And it weren't long before he had her sold. But he done as good as he could anytime. He was like me,

Haynie Marshall building a skiff at the Tylerton waterfront, April 8, 1994.

he didn't fail to nail 'em [build a sturdy boat] . . . as good as he could."

Another builder of wooden skiffs still resides in Tylerton, Smith Island's most remote community. Waterman Haynie Marshall estimates he has built twenty-four flat-bottomed skiffs in the 16- to 19-foot range for people at Smith and Tangier Islands. A few years ago he also built a skiff for a man from "Save the Bay," the local moniker for the Chesapeake Bay Foundation, which maintains an educational field station in Tylerton.

Marshall's wooden skiffs are easy to spot, with their spacious, longitudinally planked foredecks, an ideal feature for "crab-netters," those watermen who pole their way over the shallow beds of eelgrass in search of soft crabs. Standing on the foredeck gives a crabber the needed height for peering into the water to find soft crabs and peelers amongst the grasses. Once the crab is spied, the netter deftly scoops it into the net attached to the other end of the pole.

Like other boatbuilders, Marshall picked up his knack for skiff-building in an informal way, by examining other skiffs and by trial and error. In explaining his aptitude for building handsome and rugged flat-bottomed skiffs, he mused, "You know how people might have talents born into them."

During a brief visit to Smith Island in April 1994, folklorist David A. Taylor and I found Haynie Marshall building a skiff at the Tylerton pier. Marshall had not built a boat in ten years, so it must have been some sort of folklorists' luck that drew us to Tylerton on that particular day. He had started the boat a couple of days earlier and expected to finish it in a few more, depending on the weather. The skiff represented his typical model: 18 feet long, with a 4-foot, 2-inch beam. Her pine keel is a salt-treated 2 × 4, and the bottom planks are 1 × 6s of Ponderosa pine fastened perpendicular to the keel, in the typical cross-planked fashion. The skiff's battens (frames) are set on 12-inch centers. All of the fastenings are bronze, except for the stainless steel drifts Marshall used to bolt the bow stem onto the stem liner. The skiff was still in the upside-down stage when we arrived, but it was clear Marshall would be summoning his neighbors soon for help in turning the hull.

This skiff was going to be Marshall's own. His other boat is a wooden box-stern, *Debbie M*, built in Deltaville, Virginia, in 1974. When he was more active in the water business, Marshall used the larger boat for oystering and crabbing; he plans to use the new skiff for fishing a few crab pots and the like. But first, Marshall intends to cover the new skiff with fiberglass, a strategy followed by many other Smith Islanders for prolonging the life of a vessel and reducing maintenance requirements. As the boat census bears out, fiberglass skiffs are, far and away, the most popular at Smith Island. Of the 136 skiffs surveyed, 83 were fiberglass, 23 were wood covered by fiberglass, 15 were metal, and 15 were still simply wood (see Appendix A).

FIBERGLASS FINDS THE FLEET

*"Now
she's as good
as new"*

Because of ill health, Leon Marsh retired from building boats, and now his son, Larry, runs the Rhodes Point boatyard mostly as a repair and maintenance yard. Nearly every day, however, Leon still rides his motor scooter down the lane to the yard, where he participates in water-business talk with the steady stream of watermen who come by. He also offers advice on particular jobs and pitches in on minor tasks, like painting a boat's name on the bow or transom. Larry hauls boats with a Travelift and arranges them in the yard's flat, open space, where he and his crew work on them. Many watermen prefer to do the work themselves, and at certain times of the year—before crabbing season in April, and before oystering begins in October—the yard is abuzz with activity. Hulls are sanded and

painted, bottoms refastened, new water-lines struck, and new wheels (propellers) installed. The relatively warm, salty water of Tangier Sound promotes significant marine growth and worm activity, requiring Smith Island's wooden boats to be hauled, scraped, and painted with copper bottom paint at least twice a year. The yard plays an important role in the community, serving as the only place on the island where watermen can get their big workboats hauled safely and have seasonal maintenance done.

Larry does not build new wooden boats himself, although he has helped his father with so many he feels he could build a crab-scraping boat or skiff if someone needed one. He is committed to living on Smith Island and being part of the water business, however, and has tried to antici-

Boat maintenance includes power-washing and
scrubbing the hull to remove barnacles and other
marine growth. The *Olive V.*'s owner, Olden
Bradshaw Sr., works the hose while Morris Bradshaw scrubs.

pate what watermen there will need and want in these rough times and those that lie ahead. But when Larry imagines the future, he doesn't see more *Darlene*s or *Louise B.*s, he sees a fleet of fiberglass vessels.

While fishermen in other regions of the United States have been working out of fiberglass boats for two decades or more, in the Chesapeake in general (and Smith Island, in particular), the switch to 'glass has been greeted with skepticism. Still, there were two progressive islanders, brothers-in-law, who took the plunge years ago. In 1975, Dwight Marshall, a waterman's waterman from Tylerton, bought a new 35-foot Bruno and Stillman, a widely known manufacturer of round-bilged, molded fiberglass workboats based in New Hampshire. Marshall had already studied and experimented with a fiberglass sheathing material called C-Flex on his own:[1]

Well, I read about fiberglass in magazines, and we did a little bit of experimenting with fiberglass on our wooden skiffs. We used to fiberglass them with the resin coating and mat C-Flex all over the wood, and we put them through a lot of ice a-hunting. [We] do a lot of duck hunting, and we'd cut through a lot of ice and it wouldn't hurt the hull any at all. We figured this would be the thing to switch to. It was getting so expensive to keep a wooden boat up, the woodwork, the carpenter work, everything, the labor and material was getting so high, and you couldn't get the lumber you wanted. Most of the lumber was not seasoned good and it would rot easy, and you'd have to be replacing lumber every so often. It was getting pretty expensive, so we figured fiberglass would be the thing to switch to.

Marshall's brother-in-law, Elmer "Junior" Evans, also bought a 35-foot Bruno and Stillman in 1975. At the time, he wasn't exactly in the market for a fiberglass boat, since he was still happily working out of his first big workboat, *Mary Ruth*, a 37-foot wooden round-stern built by Lawson Tyler, in Ewell, in 1960. While attending a trade show in Ocean City, however, he had the chance to try out a new fiberglass model, and it changed his mind. He was amazed at how she handled in rough seas and was convinced on the spot that fiberglass was the way to go. Twenty years later, *Miss Sherry* is still his boat of choice. She is round bilged and, therefore, of deeper draft than *Mary Ruth*, but since Evans uses her for crab potting, he doesn't need to work in the shallows as do scraping boats. Her higher bow has also eliminated one of the major problems he encountered eight or nine times with *Mary Ruth*: broken cabin windows caused by water crashing over her bow. Because of *Miss Sherry*'s high bow, he has never had such troubles since. Like many watermen, however, Evans has not forgotten his first workboat. During the winter when he has some spare time, he builds boat models, and one of the first he made was of the round-stern *Mary Ruth*. The model occupies a prominent place in the Evans home.[2]

Eddie Evans, Junior's brother, held out for a decade before investing in a new fiberglass workboat in the mid-1980s:

It got so that a boat carpenter was getting hard to come by, and if you had a wooden boat, it was getting [to be] a job to find people that really knowed how to work on a wooden boat. I mean, it's a lot of difference between a house carpenter and a boat carpenter. I mean, anybody that's going to work on a boat, a wooden boat, has really got to know how to fit wood. It's nothing square and you've got to do it all by just chopping out, making it fit, and that was a vanishing trade. And people could see it was getting so it was costing so much money for to upkeep a wooden boat, that when fiberglass first started coming along, why, people was skeptical of it because they didn't think, like anything else, you've been used to it all of your life with wood, somebody comes along and says, "fiberglass," you know, you've got to see it proved out. But it's proved out real well, it's low maintenance, and it's something that was needed at the time.

For Julian "Juke" Bradshaw Sr., fiberglass seemed to work miracles when it gave new life to an old wooden skiff he had abandoned and given up for dead in the marsh:

I have a small skiff, 16-foot skiff with a Johnson outboard on her. She's wood covered with 'glass. In fact, the ice busted her a few years ago [before she was covered with fiberglass]. I had to even turn her loose, because it would cost me a lot of money to — I'd had to put a whole new side in it. But when fiberglass come out, I went back and found her. She went over here on the marsh. I went back and I redone her. I took that bad piece out of her, the bust out of her, and then I refiberglassed her inside and out. Now she's as good as new. She don't leak a drop.

Haynie Marshall built it [the skiff] for me when I had it built. I've had it built a right good while, but like I said, when that ice busted her, it busted her side in, and she always would leak. But when fiberglass come out, you can redo them kind of boats now. I'd lost her, but after they got doing old skiffs and old boats — in fact, I'm going to do my big boat sometime if I live, you know, and I ever get able to do it. It costs a lot of money to do it, but I'm going to have it done, because I'll have then another new boat, just about.

For Larry Marsh, the idea of fiberglass took hold several years ago when a neighbor hauled his big workboat at the boatyard and began C-Flexing the hull, as Dwight Marshall and "Juke" Bradshaw had done to their skiffs. Everyone hanging around the boatyard watched the process with interest. When it became clear that the project would culminate in a refurbished vessel virtually equivalent to a new boat, one that would require less upkeep, other watermen wanted the same thing done to their aging wooden hulls. Few watermen today can afford a new boat, and they believe they can get several more working years out of their old wooden boats with C-Flex.[3] Training in the C-Flex technique for Larry and the boatyard crew has been eased by another form of new technology: a four-hour instructional video can be purchased from the company that markets the product.[4] Thus, the basic techniques for applying this material to a wooden hull can be absorbed in a matter of hours or days. This is in stark contrast to learning how to build wooden boats the traditional way — by watching and practicing with an elder, making mistakes, and eventually developing your own "model" within the parameters of the local design tradition.

Still, C-Flexing an old, wooden hull is time consuming and offers any number of chances for costly errors. First, the hull must be leveled and stripped of all hardware, guard rails, and toe rails. If there is any rot in the planking, it has to be replaced. The hull is then sanded down to the bare wood and "plastered" with C-Bond, a moisture-cured polyurethane substance that seals the cracks and helps bond the C-Flex to the hull. Next, the C-Flex is laid in vertical sheets from the sheer to the keel and stapled in place with 1⅛-inch stainless steel staples. An astonishing twenty thousand staples are used to C-Flex a 43-foot-long hull. The next step requires saturating the C-Flex with a coating of a polyester resin. When the resin cures, the hull is sanded, then "flood coated" with more resin. A layer of chopped fiberglass mat is laid down next, then rolled to remove air bubbles. The mat is then sanded, and a second layer of fiberglass mat is applied. Certain areas of the hull—the garboard area on both sides

of the keel and the chines—receive extra layers of matting for additional protection. The hull is then faired with fiberglass "microspheres," or what Larry Marsh calls "the bubbles." This substance is spread carefully onto the hull for a smooth surface. After a final sanding of the entire hull, four layers of gelcoat are sprayed on for a hard finish.[5]

Elmer "Junior" Evans aboard his fiberglass workboat *Miss Sherry*, a round-bilged boat he finds ideal for crab potting. *Miss Sherry* was manufactured by the Bruno and Stillman Company in New Hampshire. She has more freeboard and deeper draft than vessels built locally.

Elmer "Junior" Evans with the model he built of his first workboat, the round-stern *Mary Ruth*. The transom of his current boat, *Miss Sherry*, is visible in the background.

In mastering these techniques, Larry has benefited from the expertise of Garrett "Joe" Kyte, a boatbuilder who moved to Smith Island in the 1940s and, for the next fifty years, produced a number of wooden and fiberglass boats. Kyte embraced fiberglass in the 1980s and never looked back. Interviewed in 1989 for *National Fisherman* magazine, he explained:

Don't get me wrong. I still like a wood boat, but materials are hard to get, and it's not handy floating those big keels way over here from Crisfield to build a boat. Times change. We had candles, then oil lamps and then electricity. Time catches up with you, and I guess fiberglass has caught up with me. You go up and down that shore, you'll see a lot of fiberglass skiffs, but when I first came here in 1942 there wasn't anything but kerosene lamps for lights, three-crank telephones and all the wooden boats in the world. Times have changed.[6]

Larry Marsh now offers C-Flexing as a service of his yard. He is less than fond of certain aspects of the procedure: the noxious fumes of the polyester resin, handling the scratchy fiberglass matting, sanding the hardened resin. His father, Leon, agrees and stays clear of the part of the building where the fiberglass operations take place; he prefers to sit back in the shop, which still smells of wood. In addition, Leon remains distrustful of fiberglass as a safe material for boats. He uttered, "I don't want no part of that. Never did. . . . No, they [fiberglass boats] don't work near as good as a wooden boat. They have 'em around here, but the wind blows 'em around." This belief—that fiberglass boats handle differently and are less stable than wooden boats—is echoed by other long-time proponents of wood. Indeed, boats of similar design made of wood or fiberglass have a different "feel" in the water because of differences in how the weight of these materials is distributed. Despite the reluctance of some, the community seems to be responding favorably to Larry's expansion. "Juke" Bradshaw remarked, "He's going to have a rig that he can [use to] fiberglass your boat even if she's fifty years old. It's going to be a big help to the watermen."

Larry has expanded his business even further, beyond saving old wooden boats by sheathing them in fiberglass. When Joe Kyte moved to the mainland in 1993, Larry purchased the set of sectional molds and frames Kyte had used in producing new, C-Flex-constructed fiberglass boats. In 1994, he launched his first new fiberglass boat produced with Kyte's old frames, *Rambler*, built for a man in Mt. Holly, Virginia. For this sort of work Larry erected a new building at the boatyard. Whereas wooden boats can be built out in the open, fiberglass construction requires an enclosed (but well-ventilated) structure to keep the materials perfectly clean and dry. Larry has even begun running ads in *Waterman's Gazette*, the monthly newspaper of the Maryland Watermen's Association, to drum up business. His ads represent the first time the Smith Island boatyard has looked to anything but the occupational grapevine for advertising.

Actually, Smith Island watermen have had the choice of buying new, locally built workboats made of molded fiberglass since 1984. Eugene Evans, a native of Rhodes Point and former waterman, moved to the mainland in the mid-1970s

Larry Marsh sanding the hull of a 43-foot boat during the process of sheathing it in fiberglass, 1993.

and established Evans Boat Construction & Repair, in Crisfield. Evans was inspired to construct his first fiberglass crab-scraping boat when his father needed a replacement for his old wooden crabber. Evans had some ideas about changes in the crab-scraping boat design, which he tried out as he translated the form to fiberglass. Using his father's old wooden boat as a plug to make a mold, he maintained the shape of the vessel forward but made several changes to the hull from amidships aft.

Evans's most significant change in the design was to the stern. Well aware of the need for settling boards on the older scraping boats, he thought he could improve even on the box-stern design by forming a tunnel drive in his fiberglass hull. The tunnel drive, a familiar feature on some fiberglass powerboats, is a long indentation (tunnel) in the stern of the hull, which houses the propeller. Adapted to Evans's scraping boat, it answers the most basic requirement of scraping by permitting the boat to work in only twelve inches of water. Evans's model also has five inches more freeboard than the tradi-

tional wooden scraping boats. Higher sides are desirable for those watermen who want to use the boat for other purposes.[7]

As one would expect, Evans is a true believer in fiberglass boats as the best choice for working watermen on the Chesapeake. The advantages, he says, far outweigh any possible disadvantages. His most compelling argument has to do with upkeep; unlike wooden boats, those of fiberglass need not be hauled twice a year for hull scraping and repainting. Nor are there bottom planks to refasten periodically. While the initial cost for a fiberglass boat used to be greater than that for wood, such is no longer the case. The cost for a new fiberglass boat is roughly comparable to wood, and over time, with reduced maintenance time and money, it becomes more cost effective. Finally, being lighter than water-soaked wood, fiberglass boats generally use less fuel, thereby adding to their overall economy.

The transition from wood to fiberglass concerns more than just materials, however. It also signals the shift from hand-crafted to mass-produced hulls, as signifi-

A fiberglass crab-scraping boat in the Tylerton

boat basin. The Somerset 26 is manufactured by

Evans Boat Construction in Crisfield.

FIBERGLASS FINDS THE FLEET

Heading into the harbor at Ewell, Tracy Kitching and his fiberglass workboat, *Rock-a-Little,* represent a new generation of watermen and workboats at Smith Island. Note *Rock-a-Little*'s flared bow. Kitching has rigged the boat for crab potting; the circular pot-hauler is visible on the starboard washboard.

THE WORKBOATS OF SMITH ISLAND

cant a change as the switch from sail- to engine-powered craft earlier in this century. The gradual acceptance of fiberglass boats at Smith Island is already having a narrowing effect on the range of variation within the Smith Island workboat fleet. The diverse aspects of traditionally conceived boat designs, which distinguish one vessel as Maryland- or Virginia-built or as "Marsh-built," "Butler-built," "Somers-built," "Capt. Lawse Tyler–built," or "Haynie Marshall–built," are simply lost when dozens of vessels pop out of the same mold. Those who live around recreational boating areas have become accustomed to the basic uniformity of fiberglass vessels mass-produced according to standardized plans. In contrast, Smith Island's current diversity of hand-crafted workboats is part of what makes the fleet unique in Maryland. Forty years ago Howard I. Chapelle lamented the beginning of this trend toward mass-produced watercraft and encouraged people to consider building traditional wooden boats, in part to "avoid the appearance of sameness that now afflicts our yachting fleets."[8] Affliction or not, it

seems likely the fleet of the future will be covered in 'glass.

Viewed from the watermen's perspective, however, the fiberglass phenomenon is entirely consistent with their occupational sense of appropriate responses to a particular set of circumstances. With so many uncertainties surrounding the future of the water business, watermen seriously weigh every monetary decision they make. And, for many, minimal upkeep over the long run eventually overpowers other factors, such as a preference for a locally built boat of a particular model, the desire to preserve woodworking skills needed for the construction and repair of wooden craft, or the ability to work with a builder to produce a custom-built vessel that reflects their own preferences. The apparent transition from wood to fiberglass in the Smith Island fleet is not for outsiders to lament, however, for the only measure that truly matters is how such decisions fulfill the occupational community's needs.[9]

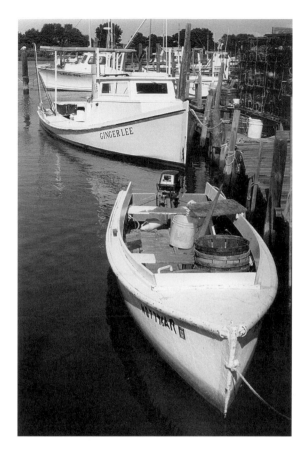

Like many all-purpose, wooden skiffs at Smith Island, the skiff in the foreground has been covered with fiberglass. The *Ginger Lee*, at her stern, is a scraping boat with an added cuddy cabin. In the distance, *Cecil Sue* is a new fiberglass model with two design features not typical of traditional workboats: a slightly flared bow and raked stem line.

A view from the past: a Smith Island waterman in
his locally built crab-scraping boat, 1965.

EPILOGUE

"Of course, I'm not figuring on leaving. I'll end my days here."

If technology (in the form of fiberglass materials) is diminishing the diversity of workboat design, other processes—historical, cultural, biological—are reducing the number of workboats altogether. As the oyster fishery continues its downward spiral, prospects dim for year-round employment on the water. A combination of related factors—pollution, overharvesting, ineffective management controls, unsuccessful natural oyster reproduction, and the terribly destructive oyster diseases MSX and dermo—has brought the Chesapeake oyster fishery to a virtual standstill. Like many seasoned watermen, Capt. Daniel Harrison, of Ewell, has witnessed cycles of abundance and scarcity in seafood resources many times before, but wonders if this time might be different:

Right now it don't look too good because the oyster is dying everywhere. Of course, I've seen them die before just like they're doing now. The only difference, it's a wider spread of it now than it was years back. I've seen it clean on back as far as in the thirties, you couldn't catch a bushel in Tangier Sound. That's the reason we go clean up to the head of Chesapeake Bay. But after a while, it changed. . . . It works in cycles. But like I say, the way it looks now, nobody is gonna know the future of it right now, because it all depends on how this disease holds on. . . . It looks bad.

Fewer young men are taking up the water business, choosing instead to pursue careers that will provide a steady income on the mainland. And even some who have worked the water for a decade or more are looking at other employment possibilities. In fall 1993, after fourteen years as a waterman, Willard Marshall, of Tylerton, told a reporter from the *Baltimore Sun* that he was seriously thinking about a land job for the first time in his life. Some of his watermen friends had already given up and become correctional officers at the state prison in Princess Anne, the Somerset County seat; perhaps he would apply for a similar position.[1] Such musings have far-reaching implications. When a Smith Island waterman takes a land job, it affects more than himself. It usually means he and his family move to the mainland, pulling up roots that are generations deep, and starting anew. Because the community of Smith Island is so closely knit, a family "moving off" the island is wrenching even for the people who remain.

Many of the community elders have no intention of leaving. They do not have young families to support and believe they can get by harvesting whatever resources the Lord provides. The strong, deep faith that sustained their forebears gives them a large measure of comfort. "Juke" Bradshaw reflected:

Well, the water business, for one thing. If it keeps going like it's going, there will be nothing here to do in the wintertime. Of course, I'm not figuring on leaving. I'm going to stay here. I'll end my days here. But the youngsters, they're going to have to find a way, you know, to make a living in the wintertime.

Now, let me say this, too. Most of our people are Christian, born-again Christian, Methodist, in fact. And we believe that the Lord has had a hand in things, and we know that if the Lord will continue to have His hand in it, we'll make out all right. There will be some way provided. We believe that, most of us do. . . . For one thing, our church, which is the main part of this community and it will always be, I believe, as long as we are a community. But we don't know. We don't know the outcome. We believe everything's going to work out all right, but we really don't know. We're hoping. We're hoping something will happen to our bay that will change things, but if it don't, we're in for a bad time, and most of us realizes that.

This faith seemed to bear fruit during the 1994–95 oyster season when the community experienced what Janice Marshall called their "Christmas miracle." After oystering up the bay in the fall, the men returned home for Christmas, as usual. To their amazement, they found healthy, legal-size oysters in nearby waters. Smith Island watermen spent the next three months working the oyster rocks in both Tangier Sound and the lower bay. Remarkably, these areas had not been planted with seed oysters by the state; the oysters they found had grown naturally on what had been deemed barren ground. Janice Marshall reported there had been "a whole lot of praying going on in these churches here," and she felt their prayers had been answered.

There is not a community in Maryland whose history and culture, whose identity and worldview, have been so shaped by the harvest of resources from the Chesapeake Bay. Likewise, there is no community whose very existence is so dependent on the bay's health. In this place, where everybody still needs a boat, the traditional nature of boat-related activity continues to flourish. Young boys still gravitate toward skiffs and learn from elders the ways of boats and the water business. Watermen still search out the perfect vessel that possesses the characteristics they value—strength, durability, economy, beauty. Meanwhile, they perpetually tinker with their gear and the way it is rigged, in case there is a better way to do their work.

Marsh's railway is still the heart of island workboat repair, especially come April and September, when the possibility of success with the new harvesting season beckons. Scraping boats and peelers, the price of soft crabs and the perils of oyster diseases, and the direction of the wind and the height of the seas are still high on the list of topics bandied about by islanders over VHF radios or in the local stores.

From the examples of *Darlene, Louise B.,* and a few unnamed skiffs, the particular ways in which Smith Islanders talk about, design, build, outfit, use, and maintain working watercraft reflects a deep understanding of their local environment, economy, and culture. That they are in the midst of changing circumstances is understood, by one and all, as well.

APPENDIX A: BOAT SURVEY

The boat survey was conducted between 1991 and 1993. Several methods were used to gather basic information about boats in use at Smith Island at the time, including a one-page questionnaire. In Ewell, Jennings Evans assisted in distributing, filling out, and collecting survey forms. In Rhodes Point and Tylerton, I interviewed individuals to gather the information. The questions as they appeared on the survey form are reproduced here.

Type of boat: (*For example,* crab-scraping boat) _____

Name of boat: (*For example,* MISS CINDY) _____

Length and beam: _____

When was this boat built? _____

Where was this boat built? _____

Who built this boat? _____

How long have you owned this boat? _____

This boat is made of: (*Please check*) Wood _____ Fiberglass _____ Wood covered with fiberglass _____ Other material (*Please name*) _____

What do you use this boat for? _____

What do you especially like or dislike about this boat? (*For example,* is she fast? pretty? sturdy?) _____

Name of person completing this survey form: _____

Name of boat owner: _____

Address and phone number: _____

May we contact you again for more information? Yes _____ No _____

In addition to requesting information by survey form, I observed as many boats at Smith Island as possible. I planned my field research to coincide with periods between harvesting seasons—April (between oystering and crabbing) and late September (between crabbing and oystering)—when most workboats were likely to be in port. With assistance from Elaine Eff, I systematically photographed boats in all three harbors, working from both land and water, when possible. These photographs were then used to elicit information from boat owners on subsequent trips.

I also frequented the L. Marsh & Son Boat Yard, at Rhodes Point, where boats are brought for maintenance, and collected data about particular boats from their owners. Back in the library, I consulted the *Merchant Vessels of the United States* volumes for 1981 and 1989, which listed registered vessels and included the larger deadrise workboats, but not scraping boats and skiffs. The *MVUS* listing provided most of the information on the questionnaire, except for individual commentary about a boat's qualities.

Since boats are a moving target, a few —especially those without names—likely escaped my notice. It is also important to note that a number of the boats tallied here can no longer be found at Smith Island. Watermen who have moved away have taken their boats with them to the mainland. Other workboats have met their demise in the intervening years.

Since 1993, several vessels deemed beyond use or salvage have been stripped of their engines and fittings before being "run up a gut" or burned at the water's edge— casualties of time and the water business. This survey, however, represents a reasonable snapshot of the fleet between 1991 and 1993.

TABLE A1   Smith Island Boat Types and Construction Materials, 1991–1993

Boat type	Wood	Fiberglass	Wood / fiberglass	Other or unknown material	Total
Crab-scraping boats	23	12	6	4	45
Round-stern deadrise	13		1		14
Box-stern deadrise	44	33	6	4	87
Skiffs	15	83	23	15	136
Specialized boats*	7	6		4	17
Total	102	134	36	27	299

*Includes the school boat, trash boat, tanker, and mail boat, as well as ferries, tour boats, buyboats, and miscellaneous pleasure craft.

TABLE A2   Place of Construction of Smith Island Workboats
(excluding Skiffs), 1991–1993

Place built	Crab-scraping boats	Round-stern deadrise	Box-stern deadrise	Total by place
Cambridge, Md.			6	6
Chance, Md.			1	1
Crisfield, Md.	5		10	15
Ewell, Md.	11		6	17
Rhodes Point, Md.	9		1	10
Rock Hall, Md.			1	1
Wingate, Md.			1	1
Amburg, Va.			1	1
Deltaville, Va.		9	22	31
Fairport, Va.			1	1
Kinsale, Va.			1	1
Norfolk, Va.			1	1
Reedville, Va.		4	1	5
Saxis, Va.	2			2
Sunnybank, Va.		1		1
Tangier, Va.			9	9
Naples, Fla.			2	2
Titusville, Fla.			1	1
Newington, N.H.			2	2
Unknown	18		20	38
Total no. of workboats	45	14	87	146

This study relied heavily on the expertise of watermen and boatbuilders at Smith Island. Whenever possible, I tried to use their words to tell the story of local workboats. The sources for quoted material are listed. "TRI" refers to tape-recorded interviews, which were conducted by Elaine Eff (EE), of the Maryland Historical Trust, and me (PJ). Field notes (FN) are notes I made of conversations that took place at Smith Island or by telephone. Information I received by letter (L) is listed as well.

Documentary materials made during and as a result of field research have been preserved. The audiotapes and transcripts are housed at the Smith Island Visitors' Center under the auspices of the Crisfield and Smith Island Cultural Alliance, Inc. Copies of the materials are on file at the Maryland Historical Trust and the Transportation Collections, National Museum of American History, Smithsonian Institution.

Name	Type	Date	Place	Interviewer/Researcher
Julian "Juke" Bradshaw Sr.	TRI	3/27/92	Tylerton	EE & PJ
Jesse Brimer Jr.	TRI	3/26/92	Ewell	EE & PJ
George M. Butler	TRI	9/24/93	Reedville	PJ
Edward A. "Eddie" Evans	TRI	3/26/92	Ewell	EE & PJ
Elmer "Junior" Evans	FN	10/7/93	Rhodes Point	PJ
Elmer "Tank" Evans	TRI	3/25/92	Ewell	EE & PJ

Eugene Evans	FN	9/10/92	Crisfield	PJ
Jeff Evans	FN	9/10/92	Ewell	PJ
Jennings Evans	TRI	3/25/92	Ewell	EE & PJ
	FN	10/6/92	Telephone	PJ
	FN	6/15/94	Ewell	PJ
Daniel Harrison	TRI	3/25/92	Ewell	EE & PJ
Michael Harrison Sr.	L	12/94		PJ
Willard Laird	FN	9/27/91	Tylerton	PJ
Larry Marsh	TRI	3/26/92	Rhodes Point	EE & PJ
	FN	9/7/93	Rhodes Point	PJ
	FN	1/20/94	Telephone	PJ
Leon Marsh	TRI	10/18/90	Rhodes Point	EE & PJ
	FN	10/5/93	Rhodes Point	PJ
	FN	1/20/94	Telephone	PJ
	FN	4/8/94	Rhodes Point	PJ
Morris Goodman Marsh	FN	9/9/93	Ewell	PJ
	FN	10/7/93	Rhodes Point	PJ
	FN	4/7/94	Ewell	PJ
	L	12/94		PJ
Dwight Marshall	TRI	3/27/92	Tylerton	EE & PJ
Haynie Marshall	FN	2/16/93	Tylerton	PJ
Janice Marshall	FN	3/17/95	Tylerton	PJ
Tim Marshall	TRI	10/18/90	Rhodes Point	EE & PJ
Jerry Pruitt	FN	2/18/93	Telephone to Tangier, Va.	PJ
Lorenzo "Rooster" and	TRI	6/15/94	Ewell	PJ
Eileen Somers	FN	4/8/94	Ewell	PJ
Bobby Tyler	FN	9/9/93	Rhodes Point	PJ

SMITH ISLAND SOURCES

NOTES

PREFACE

1. Among the articles and books that feature Smith Island are: William B. Cronin, "Smith Island," *Chesapeake Bay Magazine* (July 1987): 59–61; Robert Deardorff, "An Island Named Smith," *Travel* (June 1964): 42–45; Frances W. Dize, *Smith Island, Chesapeake Bay* (Centreville, Md.: Tidewater Publishers, 1990); Tom Horton, *Bay Country* (Baltimore: Johns Hopkins University Press, 1987); Tom Horton, "A Place in the Heart," *Mid-Atlantic Country* (Jan. 1990): 28; Tom Horton, "The Chesapeake Crab Wars," *Mid-Atlantic Country* (Aug. 1992): 26–31, 78; Tom Horton, "Chesapeake Bay: Hanging in the Balance," *National Geographic Magazine* (June 1993): 4–35; Frances Kitching and Susan Stiles Dowell, *Mrs. Kitching's Smith Island Cookbook* (Centreville, Md.: Tidewater Publishers, 1981); William W. Warner, *Beautiful Swimmers: Watermen, Crabs, and the Chesapeake Bay* (Boston: Little, Brown & Co., 1976); Dan White, *Crosscurrents in Quiet Water: Portraits of the Chesapeake* (Dallas: Taylor Publishing Co., 1987); Bernard Wolf, *Amazing Grace: Smith Island and the Chesapeake Watermen* (New York: Macmillan Publishing Co., 1986). Smith Island has also been featured in films and television programs, including *The Sailing Oystermen* (CBS News Documentary for the Twentieth Century Series, 1965); *Chesapeake Borne* (National Geographic Society and WQED-TV Pittsburgh, 1985); and *Outdoors Maryland: On the Chesapeake* (Owings Mills: Maryland Public Television, 1993).

2. Field research into southern Maryland workboats and their builders was carried out in 1981–83 as part of the Patuxent River Folklife and Oral History Project, sponsored by the Calvert Marine Museum (CMM) in Solomons, Maryland, and funded by a grant from the National Endowment for the Arts. This research resulted in the permanent exhibition, *Built to Work: Building Deadrise Workboats in Southern Maryland*, at CMM.

3. For a discussion of Mr. Chapelle's career and a complete bibliography of his writings, see JoAnn Jeanelle King, "Howard I. Chapelle: Maritime Scholar and His Contribution to Maritime Preservation" (Ph.D. diss., George Washington University, 1985). See also Peter H. Spectre, "The Legacy of Howard Chapelle," *Nautical Quarterly* (Winter 1987): 110–23, and Spectre's "Legacy of Howard Chapelle: The Study of the Maritime Past, the Preservation of the Maritime Present," *WoodenBoat* 84 (Sept. / Oct. 1988): 76–88.

4. The National Watercraft Collection is the Smithsonian Institution's collection of rigged ship models, builders' half-hull models, ship design drawings, and documentation drawings of historic American watercraft. See Howard I. Chapelle, *The National Watercraft Collection*, 2nd ed. (Washington, D.C., and Camden, Me.: Smithsonian Institution Press and International Marine Publishing Co., 1976) for a catalog of the collection.

SMITH ISLAND, MARYLAND: WHERE EVERYBODY NEEDS A BOAT

1. See M. V. Brewington, *Chesapeake Bay Log Canoes and Bugeyes* (Cambridge, Md.: Cornell Maritime Press, 1963); Robert H. Burgess, *Chesapeake Sailing Craft, Part I* (Cambridge, Md.: Tidewater Publishers, 1975); Howard I. Chapelle, "Chesapeake Bay Crabbing Skiffs," pts. 1 and 2, *Yachting* (June 1943): 41–43, 76–78, and (Oct. 1943): 33–35, 58–60; Howard I. Chapelle, "Notes on Chesapeake Bay Skipjacks," *American Neptune* (Oct. 1944): 269–303; Howard I. Chapelle, *American Small Sailing Craft: Their Design, Development,*

and Construction (New York: W. W. Norton and Co., 1951); Richard J. S. Dodds and Pete Lesher, eds., *A Heritage in Wood: The Chesapeake Bay Maritime Museum's Small Craft Collection* (St. Michaels, Md.: Chesapeake Bay Maritime Museum, 1992); Thomas C. Gillmer, *Working Watercraft: A Survey of Surviving Local Boats of America and Europe* (Camden, Me.: International Marine Publishing Co., 1972); Quentin Snediker and Ann Jensen, *Chesapeake Bay Schooners* (Centreville, Md.: Tidewater Publishers, 1992).

2. Frances W. Dize, *Smith Island, Chesapeake Bay* (Centreville, Md.: Tidewater Publishers, 1990): 53.

3. Adam Wallace, *The Parson of the Islands: The Life and Times of the Rev. Joshua Thomas* (1861; reprint, Cambridge, Md.: Tidewater Publishers, 1978). For a discussion of Methodism at Smith Island, see Dize, *Smith Island*, 53–57, 119–22.

4. See Appendix B for sources of quoted material from Smith Islanders.

5. Until recently, Smith Island children attended school in Ewell or Tylerton through the sixth grade. In June 1996, the Tylerton school closed. The few remaining pupils from Tylerton will begin taking a boat to Ewell for classes. For grades seven through twelve, students travel to and from Crisfield every day by boat. The "school boat" in the early 1990s was *Betty Jo Tyler*, a 50-foot aluminum-hulled vessel that can carry up to fifty people. The vessel's owner, Rhodes Point native Alan Tyler, commissioned the boat from a New Orleans shipyard in 1974 and named her for his daughter.

6. Henry Hall, *Report on the Ship-Building Industry of the United States,* 10th Census (Washington, D.C.: Government Printing Office, 1884), 34.

7. Tom Horton and William M. Eichbaum, *Turning the Tide: Saving the Chesapeake Bay* (Washington, D.C.: Island Press, 1991), 115–18; Sarah L. Roberts, "Oyster Harvest Even Lower Than Anticipated; Seeding Program Postponed," *Waterman's Gazette* (May 1993): 17; Bill Gifford, "Shell Shock," *Washington Post Magazine,* 27 March 1994, 18–28.

8. The approach taken in this study was influenced by such works as David A. Taylor, *Boat Building in Winterton, Trinity Bay, Newfoundland,* Canadian Centre for Folk Culture Studies, paper no. 41 (Ottawa: National Museums of Canada, 1982); Janet C. Gilmore, *The World of the Oregon Fishboat: A Study in Maritime Folklife* (Ann Arbor, Mich.: UMI Research Press, 1986); C. Richard K. Lunt, "Lobsterboat Building on the Eastern Coast of Maine: A Comparative Study" (Ph.D. diss., Indiana University, 1976); and Richard Lunt, "Crafting the Model: Maine Lobsterboat Building as a Design Tradition," in *By Land and by Sea: Studies in the Folklore of Work and Leisure, Honoring Horace P. Beck on His Sixty-fifth Birthday,* ed. Roger D. Abrahams, Kenneth S. Goldstein, and Wayland D. Hand (Hatboro, Penn.: Legacy Books, 1985), 141–66.

9. For full descriptions of standard documentation procedures, see Richard K. Anderson Jr., *Guidelines for Recording Historic Ships* (Washington, D.C.: National Park Service, U.S. Department of the Interior, Historic American Engineering Record, 1988), and Paul Lipke, Peter Spectre, and Benjamin A. G. Fuller, eds., *Boats: A Manual for their Documentation* (Nashville: American Association for State and Local History

and the Museum Small Craft Association, 1993).

10. For discussions of an ethnographic approach to documentation of watercraft, see David A. Taylor, *Documenting Maritime Folklife: An Introductory Guide,* Publications of the American Folklife Center, no. 18 (Washington, D.C.: Library of Congress, 1992), and Paula J. Johnson and David A. Taylor, "Beyond the Boat: Documenting the Cultural Context," in Lipke, Spectre, and Fuller, *Boats,* 337–56.

11. For a discussion of the importance of boat ownership to identity and status in another Chesapeake Bay community, see Carolyn Ellis, *Fisher Folk: Two Communities on Chesapeake Bay* (Lexington: University Press of Kentucky, 1986), 57–58.

12. Carolyn Ellis quotes women remarking on the boat-handling skills of a girl who ferried school children between islands: "'Does it just like a man. It's unbelievable,' a few women said in amazement." Ibid. 58. See also Andrew Lee Habermacher, "Work and Health of the Chesapeake Bay Commercial Fishermen of Somerset County, Maryland: 'It's a Hard Life, Honey!'" (Ph.D. diss., University of Florida, 1986), 97–98, 136, regarding the use of boats among Smith Island women and children.

13. Glenn Lawson, *The Last Waterman* (Crisfield, Md.: Crisfield Publishing Company, 1988), 16.

14. Frances Kitching and Susan Stiles Dowell, *Mrs. Kitching's Smith Island Cookbook* (Centreville, Md.: Tidewater Publishers, 1981), 90.

15. For a discussion of boat naming practices among Oregon fishermen, see Gilmore, *The World of the Oregon Fishboat,* 109–13; for naming and

launching traditions among Yugoslavian, Italian, and Portuguese fishermen in California, see Wayland D. Hand, "The Folk Beliefs and Customs of San Pedro's Fishermen," in *By Land and by Sea*, Abrahams, Goldstein, and Hand, 125–26; and for general information on naming traditions in various maritime communities, see Horace Beck, *Folklore and the Sea* (Middletown, Conn.: Wesleyan University Press, 1973), 18–21. The fisherman's tradition of naming his boat after a female member of his family is in marked contrast to names bestowed on modern pleasure boats. According to a survey conducted by Boat-U.S., an association of boat owners in the United States, the top ten names for boats in 1993 were *Serenity, Obsession, Osprey, Fantasea, Liquid Asset, Therapy, Seaduction, Happy Hours, Solitude,* and *Wet Dream.* Reported by Peter H. Spectre, "On the Waterfront," *Wooden-Boat* 115 (Nov. / Dec. 1993): 25.

16. The story of Bartimaeus is found in the Bible, Mark 10:46–52:

And they came to Jericho; and as he was leaving Jericho with his disciples and a great multitude, Bartimaeus, a blind beggar, the son of Timaeus, was sitting by the roadside. And when he heard that it was Jesus of Nazareth, he began to cry out and say, "Jesus, Son of David, have mercy on me!" And many rebuked him, telling him to be silent; but he cried out all the more, "Son of David, have mercy on me!" And Jesus stopped and said, "Call him." And they called the blind man, saying to him, "Take heart; rise, he is calling you." And throwing off his mantle he sprang up and came to Jesus. And Jesus said to him, "What do you want me to do for you?" And the blind man said

to him, "Master, let me receive my sight." And Jesus said to him, "Go your way; your faith has made you well." And immediately he received his sight and followed him on the way.

17. For discussions of similar taboos among fishing people of other regions, see Beck, *Folklore and the Sea,* 17–18, and Patrick B. Mullen, *I Heard the Old Fishermen Say: Folklore of the Texas Gulf Coast* (Austin: University of Texas Press, 1978), 157.

18. The feminine pronoun has been used in reference to ships and boats since the time of Homer. For example:

You need not linger over going to sea.
I sailed beside your father in the old days,
I'll find a ship for you, and help you sail her.
Hom. *Od.* 2.284–86

CRAB-SCRAPING BOATS

1. Howard I. Chapelle, "Chesapeake Bay Crabbing Skiffs," pt. 2, *Yachting* (Oct. 1943): 58.

2. Mr. Somers further explained the liming process: a waterman would put his sails in an old skiff and fill it with water. He then "slacked the lime" (mixed it with the water) and would "get in there with clean boots on and tread them down and let them stay so long." He then removed the sails from the skiff and spread them on the grass to dry.

3. Most of Howard I. Chapelle's drawings are in the Transportation Collections, Division of the History of Technology, National Museum of American History, Smithsonian Institution, Washington, D.C. Some are also in the collections of the Chesapeake Bay Maritime Museum, St. Michaels, Md.

4. Chapelle, "Chesapeake Bay Crabbing Skiffs," 35.

5. Engine power is also needed for outrunning officers of the Virginia Marine Resources Commission when Smith Islanders are occasionally found to be scraping illegally over the state line. See Tom Horton, "The Chesapeake Crab Wars," *Mid-Atlantic Country* (Aug. 1992): 26–31, 78.

6. Henry Hall remarked on this aspect of Chesapeake Bay boatbuilding in his *Report on the Ship-Building Industry of the United States,* 10th Census (Washington, D.C.: Government Printing Office, 1884), 35: "The builders hew out their boats with no other guides than the eye, sometimes aided by a rough draft on a piece of paper."

7. William W. Warner, *Beautiful Swimmers: Watermen, Crabs, and the Chesapeake Bay* (Boston: Little, Brown & Co., 1976), 208.

8. Attempts to determine the exact species of pine proved surprisingly difficult. Historically, longleaf yellow pine (*Pinus palustris*) was preferred, but such wood is no longer available locally. There are still sources for true longleaf yellow pine in North Carolina and Georgia, but prices have become prohibitively expensive for the quantities needed to build a workboat. Leon Marsh simply calls the wood he uses "Eastern Shore" yellow pine and knows of no other term for the wood. The most likely species is loblolly (*Pinus taeda*), which grows well in the southern Eastern Shore counties of Maryland and Virginia.

9. See Robert M. Steward, *Boatbuilding Manual,* 3d ed. (Camden, Me.: International Marine Publishing Company, 1987), 28–30. According to Steward, the moisture content of a newly cut tree can equal as much as half its weight. Seasoning is the process of reducing the amount of moisture

90

in the wood. The optimum moisture content for boatbuilding material is about 15 percent.

10. For a discussion of bottom-planking methods in V-bottom construction, see Howard I. Chapelle, *Boatbuilding: A Complete Handbook of Wooden Boat Construction* (New York: W. W. Norton and Co., 1941), 280–82.

11. For further discussion of forefoot construction in Chesapeake boatbuilding see Chapelle, *Boatbuilding,* 39–40, 295–98; Chapelle, "Notes on Chesapeake Bay Skipjacks," *American Neptune* (Oct. 1944): 273–74; and Chapelle, *American Small Sailing Craft: Their Design, Development, and Construction* (New York: W. W. Norton and Co., 1951), 315–16.

12. For narrative descriptions of Morris Goodman Marsh's work day scraping crabs, see Warner, *Beautiful Swimmers,* 203–37, and Mark E. Jacoby, *Working the Chesapeake: Watermen on the Bay* (College Park: Maryland Sea Grant College, 1991), 61–71. For a description of crab scraping with another Smith Island waterman, Capt. Edward Harrison, see Larry S. Chowning, *Harvesting the Chesapeake: Tools and Traditions* (Centreville, Md.: Tidewater Publishers, 1990), 217–28.

13. Warner, *Beautiful Swimmers,* 210.

14. This tradition has been widely documented. See, for example, Chapelle, "Notes on Chesapeake Bay Skipjacks," 280; George Carey, *A Faraway Time and Place: Lore of the Eastern Shore* (Washington and New York: Robert B. Luce, 1971), 182–83; and Frances W. Dize, *Smith Island, Chesapeake Bay* (Centreville, Md.: Tidewater Publishers, 1990), 140.

DEADRISE WORKBOATS

1. Randolph Norton, *Old Days on the Chesapeake and in Deltaville, Virginia* (Matthews, N.C.: Cedar Press, 1991), 13–16.

2. See Howard I. Chapelle, "Some American Fishing Launches," in *Fishing Boats of the World,* ed. Jan-Olof Traung (London: Fishing News [Books], 1955), 8–10; Thomas C. Gillmer, *Working Watercraft: A Survey of Surviving Local Boats of America and Europe* (Camden, Me.: International Marine Publishing Co., 1972), 48; and Richard J. S. Dodds and Pete Lesher, eds., *A Heritage in Wood: The Chesapeake Bay Maritime Museum's Small Craft Collection* (St. Michaels, Md.: Chesapeake Bay Maritime Museum, 1992), 47, 65–66.

3. Larry S. Chowning, "From Draketails to Potpie Sterns: Chesapeake Watermen Appreciate a Nicely Shaped Rear End," *National Fisherman Yearbook,* 1985, 78–80; Larry S. Chowning, *Chesapeake Legacy: Tools and Traditions* (Centreville, Md.: Tidewater Publishers, 1995), 194; Chapelle, "Some American Fishing Launches," 8.

4. In addition to the design plans of *Louise B.*'s stern construction in this study, see Howard I. Chapelle, *Boatbuilding: A Complete Handbook of Wooden Boat Construction* (New York: W. W. Norton and Co., 1941), 222–23, and Harry V. Sucher, *Simplified Boatbuilding: The V-Bottom Boat* (New York: W. W. Norton and Co., 1974), 218–27, for descriptions and drawings of round-stern construction.

5. Chowning, *Chesapeake Legacy,* 194.

6. See Richard C. Goertemiller, "The Sinking of the *Glenna Fay:* A Waterman's Tale of Peril and

Survival," *Chesapeake Bay Magazine* (Oct. 1992): 26–27. Goertemiller reports that *Glenna Fay* sank one October morning, after encountering a 25-knot wind out of the north. Her owner, Ray Rogers, of Reedville, had tied her broadside to several poles of his pound net. As the water churned, she bounced and snapped off a pole near her stern. The boat continued to bounce and fell heavily on top of the stump, punching a hole through the bottom. As the boat sank, the mate, who was standing by in a skiff, rescued the captain. The following day they were able to refloat *Glenna Fay;* they towed her to the marine railway, where she was repaired and put back into service.

7. Howard I. Chapelle, "Notes on Chesapeake Bay Skipjacks," *American Neptune* (Oct. 1944): 278.

8. Larry S. Chowning, "Long Wait for a New Boat Pays Off," *National Fisherman* (Dec. 1992): 59.

9. Larry Chowning, "Alton Smith and Edward Diggs: Legends of Chesapeake Bay," *National Fisherman* (Oct. 1991): 45.

10. Janice Marshall has organized a group of Smith Islanders to perform such numbers for community celebrations and local fundraisers. Dressed as country-and-western singers, members of the Smith Island Players sing the special lyrics to a karaoke tape.

11. For a good description of a day's patent-tonging on the Chesapeake Bay, see Mark E. Jacoby, *Working the Chesapeake: Watermen on the Bay* (College Park: Maryland Sea Grant College, 1991), 107–17.

12. Patent-tongers occasionally find treasures from the deep, and many a Smith Island waterman has a shelf at home where shark's teeth and other

Miocene fossils tonged up from the bottom of the bay are proudly displayed.

13. The unusual name *Rogatorro* derives from a combination of the original owner's children's names.

SKIFFS

1. Skiffs are to today's Smith Islanders what log canoes were to their ancestors two hundred years ago, when Joshua Thomas carried out his ministry as "Parson of the Islands." Thomas's biographer noted, "On the islands where his boyhood was spent, the canoe is an indispensable convenience in every family. The land is so interwoven with creeks, and cut up with water courses, that in many places a visit to one's next door neighbor can not be paid without the necessary canoe. Neither can the people attend Divine worship, or perform their ordinary business and intercourse without it. What the cart or carriage is to residents on the main, the canoe is to the islander." Adam Wallace, *The Parson of the Islands: The Life and Times of the Rev. Joshua Thomas,* (1861; reprint, Cambridge, Md.: Tidewater Publishers, 1978), 56.

2. According to museum records, the skiff was actually the first artifact given to the Crisfield Museum, on 1 June 1975, by Mr. N. Edward Insley, of Crisfield. In 1986 the Crisfield Museum donated the skiff to the Calvert Marine Museum.

3. David A. Taylor, "A Survey of Traditional Systems of Boat Design Used in the Vicinity of Trinity Bay, Newfoundland, and Hardangerfjord, Norway" (Ph.D. diss., Memorial University of Newfoundland, 1989), 14.

4. Richard J. S. Dodds and Pete Lesher, eds., *A Heritage in Wood: The Chesapeake Bay Maritime Museum's Small Craft Collection* (St. Michaels, Md.: Chesapeake Bay Maritime Museum, 1992), 50–53.

5. Howard I. Chapelle, "Chesapeake Bay Crabbing Skiffs," pt. 1, *Yachting* (June 1943): 78. Hall also noted the popularity of these speed boats at Smith Island in his study of Tangier Island, Virginia: "The types of boats on Smith Island are the same as on Tangier except that this Island has a uniform type of six horse-power speedboat which is so common that it almost replaces the small bateau found on Tangier." S. Warren Hall III, *Tangier Island: A Study of an Isolated Group* (Philadelphia: University of Pennsylvania Press, 1939), 107.

6. See Howard I. Chapelle, *American Small Sailing Craft: Their Design, Development, and Construction* (New York: W. W. Norton and Co., 1951), 315, 331–32.

FIBERGLASS FINDS THE FLEET: "NOW SHE'S AS GOOD AS NEW"

1. C-Flex was invented and developed by Seeman Fiberglass, of Harahan, Louisiana, in the 1970s. C-Flex planking consists of rigid fiberglass rods bound together with continuous fiberglass rovings and a light fiberglass cloth. C-Flex can be used to sheath a wooden hull, as well as to build a new hull by stretching it over a framework of sectional molds, which are eventually removed. These procedures contrast with a more widely known method of fiberglass construction, in which a fiberglass "female" mold is made using an existing boat as a "male" plug. Once the plug is removed from the mold, the mold can be reused numerous times. Fiberglass material is spread inside the mold and, when it has hardened, the resulting "molded fiberglass" boat hull is removed.

2. Terry Zug documented the work of several North Carolina watermen who also build boat models. See Charles G. Zug III, *Little Boats: Making Ship Models on the North Carolina Coast* (Beaufort and Boone: North Carolina Maritime Museum and North Carolina Folklore Society, 1991).

3. Roughly speaking, in 1990 the cost of a new 42-foot wooden boat was about forty thousand dollars, excluding the engine, which could add another twelve to twenty thousand dollars. At the same time, a new molded 42-foot fiberglass boat cost around seventy thousand dollars (engine included). To C-Flex a 40-foot wooden workboat would cost around twelve thousand dollars, and it is still too early to tell how many more years the C-Flex will add to the life of a boat. To finance any of these options, the typical Smith Island waterman would have to take out a bank loan. Used wooden boats offered for sale in the *Waterman's Gazette* around this same time ranged from thirty-nine hundred dollars for a 44-foot vessel to twenty-five thousand dollars for a thirteen-year-old 38-footer complete with oyster patent-tonging gear. With used boats, much depends on age and condition in determining value. Annual maintenance bills for wooden workboats vary widely, depending on the age and general condition of the boat, how much work the owner does himself, and how much he leaves to the yard crew or to other specialists, such as engine mechanics. Wooden boats are generally hauled twice a year. Owners of fiberglass boats, however, typically haul their boats once a year and do not face the chores of scraping,

painting, and repair so necessary with wooden vessels.

4. Available from Sintes F / G Designs, in New Orleans, the set of two two-hour tapes cost one hundred and twenty dollars in 1991.

5. Michael Crowley, "Sheathing an Old Wooden Boat," *National Fisherman* (Nov. 1993): 42–44.

6. Larry S. Chowning, "C-Flex System Sparks Maryland Builders' Shift to Fiberglass," *National Fisherman* (June 1989): 68.

7. Joe Valliant, "Maryland Builder Tailors 'Crab Scraper' for the Shallows," *National Fisherman* (Feb. 1986): 52.

8. Howard I. Chapelle, *American Small Sailing Craft: Their Design, Development, and Construction* (New York: W. W. Norton and Co., 1951), 4. Also see C. Richard K. Lunt, "Lobsterboat Building on the Eastern Coast of Maine: A Comparative Study" (Ph.D. diss., Indiana University, 1976), and Maynard Bray, "Before They're Gone: Recording the Maine Lobsterboats," *WoodenBoat* 115 (1993): 64–70, for discussions of this issue in relation to the diversity of designs among traditional wooden lobsterboats of Maine.

9. David B. Bowes, "Island in Time," *Mid-Atlantic Country* (Aug. 1991): 24–31, 50, touches on this subject in describing how some visitors to Tangier Island were disappointed to discover that such practical products as aluminum siding and chain-link fencing had replaced the clapboarding and picket fencing that had contributed to the island's "quaintness" in the past.

EPILOGUE

1. Rob Hiaasen, "The Waterman's Disappearing Act," *Baltimore Sun*, 29 October 1993, 1E–2E.

GLOSSARY

Aft: Toward, near, or in the stern (back end) of the boat.

Amidships: In or near the middle of the boat.

Athwartships: Across the boat, from side to side.

Bar cat: A traditional sailing crab-scraping boat.

Bateau: On the Chesapeake Bay, a skipjack or sailing crab-scraping boat of V-bottom construction, larger than a skiff.

Battens: At Smith Island, the structural frames running from the chine to the sheer clamp on a boat; what builders elsewhere call "frames." More widely known among boatbuilders as a thin, flexible strip of wood or other material used for fairing a curve, such as the sheer line.

Bay-built: On the Chesapeake Bay, a V-bottom power boat larger than a skiff.

Beam: 1. The width of the boat at its widest part. 2. At Smith Island, also the heavy timbers in deadrise boats set perpendicular to the keel and running from chine to chine to stiffen the hull. Beams are generally installed aft of the cabin and to support both ends of the engine bed. Such beams are supported by right-angle timbers known as "knees." Beams are known elsewhere in the Chesapeake Bay region as "strongbacks."

Bends: Thick planking beneath the guard running from stem to stern on the side of a vessel.

Booby house: Small, removable house that shelters the forward area of the deck on crab-scraping boats. Most of the older scraping boats built at Smith Island had booby houses, which were ideal for storing miscellaneous gear. According to Michael Harrison Sr., of Ewell, the booby house also served as a place for young boys to keep dry and to sleep when accompanying their elders on a day's scraping.

Bow: Forward end of the boat.

Box-stern: A boat with a flat, squared-off transom, or the design of the stern itself. The box-stern is currently the most popular transom design among Chesapeake Bay watermen, supplanting the round-stern workboat popular from the 1940s through the 1970s.

Brogan: On the Chesapeake Bay, an historic boat type of log construction, used for oystering and crabbing in the late nineteenth and early twentieth centuries. The brogan was larger than a log canoe and smaller than a bugeye, with a hull built of five or seven logs; its rig was similar to a bugeye's, with two masts and jib-headed sails.

The brogan was partially decked and had a small cuddy cabin forward.

Bugeye: The largest of the log-bottom vessels built on the Chesapeake Bay. The bugeye was built of seven or nine logs and used for dredging oysters and hauling freight in the late nineteenth and early twentieth centuries. Bugeyes had two masts and jib-headed sails; they were fully decked and had a large cabin aft. Bugeyes built around the turn of the century and later were frame built, retaining the round-bilged hull form, but often incorporating a round stern instead of the sharp stern of the log-built model.

Buster: A peeler crab that has started shedding (or busting out of) its hard shell to grow.

Buyboat: Any large boat used for buying oysters directly from watermen on the oystering grounds, which then hauls the oysters to shucking houses ashore. Schooners, bugeyes, and other large sailing craft served as early buyboats. Some such vessels were later converted to power for plying their trade. Buyboats built for power were generally of cross-planked, V-bottom construction with a round stern and pilot house aft. Few buyboats currently operate on the

Chesapeake; most oystermen sell their harvest to buyers ashore, who haul the oysters to shucking houses in trucks.

C-Flex: Fiberglass planking that consists of rigid fiberglass rods bound together with unsaturated strands of continuous fiberglass rovings and a light fiberglass cloth. Used to sheath wooden boats to extend their usefulness; also used to build new fiberglass boats by using the material as planking over an open framework of sectional molds, which are removed when construction is complete. C-Flex was invented and developed by Seeman Fiberglass, of Harahan, Louisiana, in the 1970s.

Chine: The intersection of the bottom and sides of a flat or V-bottom boat. In the Chesapeake Bay region, often pronounced "chime."

Chine log: The timber running from stem to stern at the chine, to which side and bottom planking are fastened; called "side keelson" at Smith Island.

Collar board: The raised framing around the deck opening; called "coaming" elsewhere.

Crab scrape: Gear used to harvest peelers and soft crabs, consisting of a triangular iron frame with a long mesh bag attached. The scrape is towed alongside a boat in the shallow waters of Tangier Sound to collect crabs in various stages of molting.

Crab-scraping boat: Shallow-draft deadrise workboat used to harvest peelers and soft crabs by towing crab scrapes through shallow, grassy waters, such as those around Smith Island. The original crab-scraping boats were sail powered and are believed to be the forerunner of the Chesapeake Bay skipjack in terms of hull form. Early crab-scraping boats looked much like scaled-down skipjacks and were even called "bateaux," a term still used at Smith Island to refer to early scrapers and skipjacks. Sailing scrapers were sometimes called "bar cats" by watermen from Tangier Island, or "Jenkins Creekers," after the name of the creek near Crisfield where many were built.

Crab shanties: Local term for the wooden structures, many of which were built on pilings over the water, that line the shores at Smith Island. Crabbers maintain a series of aerated tanks in these shanties for "shedding out" soft crabs. Peelers are sorted into various holding tanks according to how far along they are in the shedding process. Once peelers have become soft crabs by shedding their shells, they are removed from the tanks and packed for market.

Cross-planked: Method of bottom construction widely used in the Chesapeake region, where the bottom planks run from the keel to the chine. Also refers to flat-bottom boats, where the bottom planks run from chine to chine.

Deadrise: The angle at which the bottom rises, from where it joins the keel, to the chine. On the Chesapeake, used interchangeably with the term "V-bottom" to describe a hard-chine vessel. A "deadrise workboat" is, thus, a workboat with a V-bottom.

Deadwood: Solid timbers in the extreme bow or stern of a vessel in places too narrow to permit framing.

Deadwood in the deadrise: At Smith Island, the thick, carved planking in the forefoot of a V-bottom vessel.

Draft: The depth of a vessel below the waterline. A boat is said to draw so much water; Chesapeake Bay vessels are shallow-draft because they do not draw a great deal of water (i.e., they do not extend very deep below the waterline).

Dump box: At Smith Island, the boxed-off washboard where the crab scrape is dumped and the contents culled.

End: Thin, narrow piece of wood used to block off a crab-scraping boat's washboards to form a dump box, where the crab scrape is emptied.

Fiberglass: Generic term for what in industrial and engineering circles is referred to as "fiberglass reinforced plastic" (FRP).

Flare: Outward spread and upward curve of the topsides as they rise from the waterline, in the bow section of a boat.

Fore / Forward: Toward the bow of the boat.

Forefoot: Area below the waterline where the stem liner meets the keel.

Freeboard: Distance between the actual water level and the boat's sheer.

Furring strips: Strips of wood or metal used when preparing a wall, ceiling, or floor for a new surface. The strips provide a level surface upon which the new surface is installed. These thin wooden strips are used by crab scrapers at Smith Island to stiffen the ends of their awnings, which are stretched over the deck to protect the waterman and his harvested crabs from the sun.

Garboard: The first plank, or strake, adjacent to the keel on a fore-and-aft planked vessel.

Gelcoat: Thin outer coat of a fiberglass hull.

Guard: Wooden rail on the outside of the wash-board, often covered with rubber hosing, that protects the side of the vessel when docked. Also known as the "rubrail."

Half-hull model: Carved wooden scale model of a vessel, used in the design process by some boatbuilders. Since the lines of boats are identical on both sides of the center line, the half-hull model, consisting of half the vessel as if it were cut longitudinally down the center, represents the lines of the entire vessel. Half-hull models were used to design bugeyes, schooners, and other large working watercraft, but are not used by traditional builders of small power workboats in the Chesapeake region today.

Hard-chine: A boat that has a sharp angle where the bottom meets the side; any boat with a flat or V-shaped bottom is a hard-chine boat.

Heartwood: Wood surrounding the center, or heart, of a tree.

Horn timber: A timber that connects the sternpost to the transom and supports the weight of an overhanging stern. At Smith Island, certain boats are said to have "upside-down horn timbers" because of their slight concave bottom at the stern, caused by the upward curve in the horn timber.

Hull: The main body of a vessel, not including cabin, hardware, or gear.

Keel: The main structural member, the backbone of a boat running lengthwise from stem to stern.

Live box: Enclosures that are either built into or set inside a crabbing boat to keep peelers and soft crabs alive. Water is continuously pumped through live boxes, which are emptied when the crabber reaches shore.

Log: Short for log rail, meaning the wooden cap on top of the sheer strake; also called "toe rail" elsewhere.

Log canoe: The smallest of the historic Chesapeake Bay log-bottom craft, constructed of one, three, or five hollowed-out logs. Log canoes were open, sharp on both ends, and sometimes had framed and planked topsides. Their one or two jib-headed spritsails, with or without a jib, were rigged on raking, unstayed masts. Log canoes were used in the eighteenth, nineteenth, and early twentieth centuries for crabbing, fishing, and hand-tonging for oysters. Some log canoes were built for racing.

Making a lick: Expression used by crab scrapers for each tow of the scrape; also used by oyster dredgers in reference to the use of overboard dredges.

Marine railway: Place where boats are hauled out of the water for maintenance and repair. Formerly, such places had wooden or iron tracks and a cable winch for hauling boats safely, thus the name "railway." Boats on the railway are said to be "on the ways." The term "railway" is still used at Smith Island to describe the L. Marsh & Son Boat Yard, where the rails are long gone, but where boats are still hauled out of the water on a modern marine Travelift.

Patent tongs: Mechanized oyster tongs patented by blacksmith Charles L. Marsh, of Solomons, Maryland, in 1887. Since the 1950s, patent tongs have been operated with hydraulics.

Peeler: A crab that is within a few days or hours of shedding its shell to grow.

Plug mold: A fiberglass mold made to the shape of a vessel or by covering an existing vessel (the plug) with fiberglass. Once the plug is removed, the mold can be reused to manufacture multiple hulls.

Plumb: Said of the bow stem when it is nearly per-pendicular to the keel of the boat.

Port: Looking forward, the left side of the boat.

Pound net: A stationary trap formed of nets sup-ported on stakes. Includes the pound head, an enclosure of small-meshed net with a netting floor; a funnel leading into the head; the false pound, a heart-shaped enclosure; and the leader, a straight wall of netting that runs from the pound head to the shore. As fish swim along shore, they are turned toward the pound by the leader and are trapped in the pound head.

Rabbet: A groove cut along the face of a timber, such as the keel, to receive the edge of a plank fitted to it.

Raisings: An additional log (toe rail) forward, as on the crab-scraping boat *Darlene*.

Rake: To slant or incline from the vertical; the amount of rake to the stem and stern of dead-rise workboats often varies between models.

Scantlings: The dimensions of individual hull members, such as frames and planks.

Settling board: A thin plywood board attached horizontally beneath and behind the transom of power workboats to prevent the stern from squatting or settling when underway. Settling boards are bolted to the transom with iron or wooden struts and are especially necessary on boat hulls with raked transoms, usually indicating a hull that has been adapted from a sailing design or a hull designed for much lower horsepower than most modern engines provide.

Sheer clamp: A timber running on the inside of the sheer plank, underneath the washboards. The top of the battens are fastened to the sheer clamp.

Sheer line: The profile of the top of the hull; the top edge of the hull. Sometimes referred to simply as the boat's "sheer."

Side keelsons: At Smith Island, the timber running from stem to stern on the inside of the planking at the chine; known elsewhere as the "chine piece" or "chine log."

Sister keelsons: At Smith Island, fore-and-aft timbers that run along the inside of the bottom from stem to stern, midway between the keel and the side keelsons, adding stiffening to the hull. More commonly known as "stringers."

Skeg: Pronounced "skag" at Smith Island and other watermen's communities on the Chesapeake Bay, refers to the deadwood connecting the keel to the sternpost. The skeg provides longitudinal stability to the vessel.

Skiff: At Smith Island, any small, open boat, usually 18 feet in length or shorter. Traditional wooden skiffs have flat, cross-planked bottoms; however, some built at Smith Island in the past had shallow, fore-and-aft planked, V-shaped hulls. More recently acquired fiberglass or metal skiffs owned by Smith Islanders are shallow V-bottom craft. Skiffs are typically powered by an out-board motor mounted on the transom. They are multipurpose vessels at Smith Island, used for transportation between communities, recreational fishing, netting for soft crabs, gunning, and exploring the marshes.

Skipjack: Sailing workboat of deadrise construction used to harvest oysters with dredges. Similar in hull form to the early crab-scraping vessels, the skipjack (also called a two-sail bateau) is larger and decked and has a cabin. Skipjacks carry a triangular mainsail and jib, set on a raking mast. Being sail-powered vessels, skipjacks can lawfully harvest oysters in Maryland using dredges, the most efficient harvesting gear. Since dredging under sail reduces the overall efficiency, this law dating to 1865 was intended to conserve the oyster resource. Maryland's skipjack fleet is the only sail-powered commercial fishing fleet in North America.

Soft crab: Crab that has just shed its shell to grow. In this state, the soft crab is entirely defenseless against all predators.

Sprung decking: A deck (or "washboard") made of narrow strips of wood that have been fitted together longitudinally. Also known as "yacht-laid," as opposed to "ship-laid," decking.

Starboard: Looking forward, the right side of a boat.

Staving: Vertical planking used in construction of some round sterns on Chesapeake workboats.

Stem: The upright, farthest forward part of the bow bolted to the stem liner. Typically made of hardwood, such as white oak. Also called the cutwater.

Stem liner: Structural member at the bow of a boat, fastened to the keel. The vessel's side planks are fastened to the stem liner.

Stern: The rear part of the boat.

Sternpost: The principal upright post at the stern of a vessel.

Strake: Planking running parallel to the keel.

Stringer: At Smith Island, similar to sister keelsons, but with smaller timbers.

Strongbacks: Heavy frames set perpendicular to the keel, which run from chine to chine to strengthen the hull of a deadrise boat. Known as "beams" among Smith Islanders.

Toe rail: See "log."

Transom: At the stern of the vessel, the flat, upright surface that connects the boat's two sides, sitting perpendicular to the center line. A vessel's name and home port are often lettered across the transom. Sharp-ended boats, like log canoes, do not have transoms.

Travelift: Gasoline-powered, wheeled device used to lift boats out of the water for maintenance and repair. Operated by a driver, the Travelift is situated to straddle both sides of a boat slip. The operator lowers the Travelift's sturdy slings into the water, and the vessel enters the slip over the slings. The operator lifts the boat in the slings out of the water and transports it to a work area, where the vessel is lowered onto blocks or other supports. When work on the vessel is completed, the process is reversed and the Travelift is employed to return the boat to the water.

Tunnel drive: Indentation (or tunnel) in the after part of a vessel's hull, which allows a waterman to use a larger "wheel" without sacrificing shallowness of draft. The "wheel" and shaft are housed in the tunnel.

Vernacular boatbuilding: Local boatbuilding traditions, including design processes and construction techniques, passed informally among members of a community.

Washboard: Decking between the log and collarboard. Dump boxes for emptying crab scrapes are formed by blocking the washboards with ends.

Waterman: On the Chesapeake Bay, the men who "follow the water," harvesting the annual round of oysters, crabs, clams, and fish for commercial markets. While people living around the bay have always harvested local resources for subsistence, it was not until the nineteenth century that watermen became an important occupational group. The development of transportation networks, refrigeration, and expanding markets in the mid-nineteenth century gave rise to the number of commercial watermen on the Chesapeake.

Wheel: A workboat's propeller.

Wormshoe: Thin, narrow strip of wood fastened to the bottom of the keel and skeg to protect them from wood-boring worms.

INDEX